New Dimensions in Teaching Children

New DIMENSIONS IN TEACHING CHILDREN

ROBERT G.
FULBRIGHT

BROADMAN PRESS
Nashville, Tennessee

ISBN: 0–8054–4917–5

Photographs by Robert Jackson

Library of Congress Catalog Card Number: 77–145980
Dewey Decimal Classification: 268.432
Printed in the United States of America

VOICES

I
Am lonely;
Filled with emptiness.
In lethargy and blind apathy,
I sit in squalor and confusion.
No hope for today or for tomorrow.
My tomorrows, a patterned replica of today's hopelessness.
In pathos and poverty I reach for answers.
Who cares enough to show me a path of hope?
Or how to sing a happy song of childhood?
Who will teach me how a child laughs?
And kindle within a spark for knowledge?
Who will teach me how to dream?
Or that someone really cares?
Who dares plant hope?
My heart waits,
And waits,
Empty.

I?
I, too,
Know real loneliness.
Surrounded by material plenty;
Oblivious to fear, want, hunger;
I thrive amidst comfort and convenience.
The hope of tomorrow, my rightful inheritance;
My bright tomorrows well-nourished with today's choice opportunity.
My knowledge born and nourished in this affluent society,
Environment shielding me from the despicable, inferior, the terrifying.
With energy and eagerness I reach for answers;
Answers which evolve not from these tangibles.
Who will teach me of myself?
To dream a real dream?
Who brings me hope?
My heart waits,
And waits,
Empty.

Voices;
Haunting voices;
Endless, haunting voices
Of American's forgotten children.
Status-seeking suburb, cradling children.
Austere, high-rise apartment, cradling children.
Appalachia, remote, accusing, cradling children.
City slum, cradling children.
Gaunt, garish ghetto
Cradling children.
Cradling.

I
Am lonely;
Filled with emptiness.
In plenty and poverty . . .
An endless circle . . .
On, on . . .
On . . .

                    Muriel F. Blackwell

From all walks of life, from all sections of America, from all stratas of society come the voices of children saying, "Take me, love me, and show me." The church has the awesome responsibility of taking children, loving children, showing children.

The Christian education of boys and girls is an imperative for the church. To that end this book is dedicated.

The need for effective Christian education with boys and girls, grades one through six, is paramount. The traditional approach used by the church for the past two or three generations will not suffice today. The book answers the question of why team teaching and pupil involvement in learning is a more desirable approach to teaching boys and girls in a church setting. The book is developed primarily for a teaching situation in a church; however the principles carry over into any teaching setting.

An attempt has been made to make this book as practical as possible by using numerous photographs and samples of work done by children in grades one through six. It has been written in a nontechnical language in an attempt to communicate with the average teacher in a church.

Appreciation is expressed to all who have had a part in the preparation and evaluation of the manuscript. Especially am I indebted to the professional workers in elementary education at the Sunday School Board, Woman's Missionary Union, and The Brotherhood Commission of the Southern Baptist Convention, to those who direct children's work in state Baptist conventions, and to the professors of childhood education at Southern Baptist seminaries. My colleagues, Eugene Chamberlain, Mrs. Muriel Blackwell, W. Mark Moore, Dan Padgett, Miss Elsie Rives, Miss Dolores Baker, Daryl Heath, and Robert Parris have contributed much to my personal growth and understanding of children and in the development of my philosophy of teaching children. And last, but not least, to my wife, Pat and my children—Todd, Lisa, Mandy and Matt—for their encouragement, interest, and love.

Robert G. Fulbright

CONTENTS

CHAPTER ONE
"WHAT IT'S ALL ABOUT"

Third-grade Timmy burst into the house out of breath following his first day in the new Dodson school and exclaimed, "Mom, you should see our school. It's different. Instead of one small room like we had last year, it is a big area. There are so many things to do! Learning will be fun this year!"

Sammy, a sixth grader, is engrossed in auditing bank accounts of the play-like bank instituted in his room at school. The subject of economics emerges with interest as he relates it to everyday life. Now Sammy knows how to deposit money, write checks, and examine a monthly bank statement.

Betty, a fifth grader, highly intrigued by technology, is searching in the card catalog for a book on jet propulsion. Having completed the two required tasks in the science center, she is now working on task three which calls for research from two additional sources on jet propulsion.

These situations are typical of the teaching and learning taking place in public schools across our nation. Children are approaching the task of learning with a new zeal—suddenly it has become exciting and challenging. The processes of thinking, analyzing, examining, and questioning have become intergal parts of our children. This is good!

That is, it is good unless these processes are being ignored or squelched at church. Children are supposed to contemplate, create, examine, build, memorize, practice, experiment, investigate, discover, learn, search.

A close look at the teaching taking place in many churches will reveal that on the whole children are not challenged as much as they are in public schools. Yet the message the church has to offer—and is compelled to give—is far more important than the subject matter taught in our schools.

To become effective teachers we must understand our learners—the children. What are the influences around them that pressure them into certain behavior patterns? How they are bombarded by TV, scouts, piano lessons, little league, public school, parents, peers . . . Because school has become such a formidable force through sheer exposure (forty of a child's most active hours a week for nine months each year), let's see what has happened in recent years . . .

The late 50's and the 60's witnessed a surge in education that brought drastic change. This change came so abruptly that the educational world is still feeling the jerk! The elementary-school teacher has been forced to become an innovator. The traditional liberal arts stance suddenly shifted to science and technology. Sputnik has been blamed for the revolution on the American scene, and yet from the revolution many thrilling and exciting things have emerged.

Mass media, another force, has influenced our society with great impact. Creative and conniving advertising on television has created million dollar markets for children's products. Suddenly the child— even the preschooler—is aware of "brands" and wants only those things about which he has learned on television. The nonreader can immediately identify cereals on the shelf in the supermarket. Mass media offers many educational influences. Vocabularies increase for the child because of his exposure to television and the radio. The small transistor radio becomes the constant companion of many children.

A mobile society uproots families and thrusts young couples into new and different environments. The seemingly stable society of the 50's has changed drastically. Values of parents and grandparents are being challenged by teen-agers and children. New situations arise which create questions about old values. "Why" is often asked by youth and children and the "why" lingers unanswered many times.

Where does this leave the church and its role in teaching the child? What is the objective of Christian education and how can it be realized? What basic principles guide the teachers and learners as truth is discovered and appropriated? What are the essential elements in a good teaching/learning situation?

The Christian educator who is serious about the task of teaching children must be aware of the influences and environment of the child. Perhaps his first step is to recognize that the environment of the child changed drastically from his own childhood environment. Some teacher may approach the task of teaching children in a manner similar to the way he was taught twenty years ago. His concept of teaching may be to gather six or eight children around him who will sit still and listen while he teaches the "lesson." Yet these same children attend public school five days a week and are taught to explore and investigate. They experience learning through real involvement—which is far more than just listening. These children who are exposed to many exciting methods will not be happy at church just listening to a teacher. The world is alive and moving! Children are a part of this movement. If the church teaches the child, the church must move forward.

Christian education differs from public school education in that through Christian education we are teaching about a way of life (attitudes, values, abstract ideas) and not just learning skills or subject matter. In order to do this we go to the Bible and introduce boys and girls to great Bible personalities, helping the pupils see how God has made a difference in the lives of these people.

There is a need for our elementary-age boys and girls to realize that these are *real* people who *really* lived and had feelings and emotions as we do. One worker achieved this idea through creative writing. The group had just finished the Bible story of Nehemiah, who led the people of Jerusalem to rebuild the wall. The teacher asked the boys and girls to pretend they lived during this time. Then each was asked to write a letter to a friend, desrcibing the situation. One fifth grader wrote:

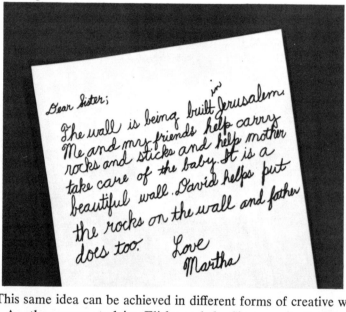

Dear Sister;

The wall is being built Jerusalem. Me and my friends help carry rocks and sticks and help mother take care of the baby. It is a beautiful wall. David helps put the rocks on the wall and father does too. Love Martha

This same idea can be achieved in different forms of creative writing. Another group studying Elisha and the Shunammite family was asked to reconstruct the story in their own words. Sometimes this is referred to as writing the Bible in your own words. One boy (sixth grader) describes 2 Kings 4:18–37 as shown on the next page.

As these individuals become real people to boys and girls, they can more easily identify with the Bible characters and sense the thrill of a life directed and guided by God.

What is the role of the church in Christian education? Each church is unique. Members in one congregation come from suburbia where many young parents and children live. Another church situated near a retirement village is composed mainly of senior citizens. The church in the inner city which ministers to children with little or no church background is vastly different from the large downtown church made up of children who have been brought to church since infancy and have been regularly taught Christian concepts in the home. Each church is different and must decide the specific objectives it is to accomplish. This decision may be reached intelligently through long-range planning and goal-setting. But unfortunately, in many churches, educational objectives have never been formally stated and exist more or less hazily only in the minds of those teaching.

As one who teaches children at church, what is your objective? Why are you teaching? If Johnny's father stopped you in the hall of your church building and asked, "What are you trying to accomplish at church as you teach Johnny," how would you answer?

The foundation of Christian education is the Bible. Through its program of Christian education, the church must relate the biblical message to the life of its learners. For the child, one of the most difficult concepts is to see the Bible as one continuous story—the revelation of God himself to man down through the centuries. The preschooler or younger elementary age child must take this revelation in small pieces. His study is usually limited to certain Bible personalities in situations that are within his range of understanding. Later in the elementary years, however, he can begin grasping larger pieces of this marvelous picture! Suddenly Susan realizes that Abraham, Isaac, Esau and Jacob, and Joseph represent four generations of the

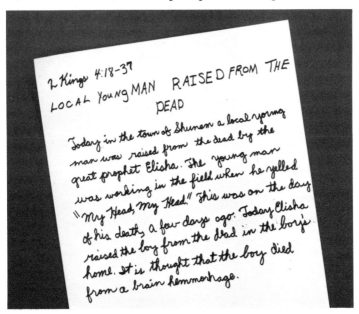

same family. And this drama intensifies as the child sees how wonderfully God worked through the lives of these four generations!

One educator has summarized the objectives of Christian education as to bring about *nurture* and *decision*.[1] The two are closely intertwined and cannot be separated. Nurture, when properly done will precipitate decision. To nurture means to educate, to train, or to bring up. In Christian education our role is to guide children in grasping (internalizing, understanding) Christian concepts. Christian education includes developing Bible-based concepts around such themes as God, Jesus, Bible, church, home, prayer, world, others, and self. This biblical foundation can naturally flow into a realization of why God reveals himself to man. At many points in his development, the child will be faced with decision. Confronting and making decisions will ultimately lead to the biggest and most important decision of his life—life commitment to God through Jesus Christ.

Another writer in summarizing the objective of Christian education for young children said:

How can we sum up what a church ought to be achieving as far as Preschoolers in its community are concerned? Most of us would immediately reply that this objective is characterized by the laying of foundations for all of the life of each child. We want each child to become a Christian when he reaches accountability [responsible decision making]. We look forward to watching each child's growth in grace after he becomes a Christian.

Is it enough to look toward the future in this manner? Or is there some element in our responsibility which is concerned with the present? Nearly any . . . worker in any church organization would respond: "Yes, the church must help the child find meaning in his present experiences." As one considers earlier efforts to state . . . objectives, he sees three major elements. In the next paragraph, these elements are combined in a tentative objective. Read the statement carefully and consider its validity for work in your own church.

A church should guide each Preschooler [and elementary age child] in experiences which help to:
- Enrich his present spiritual growth.

---

[1] G. Campbell Wycoff, address at the Southern Baptist Religious Education Association, Denver, Colorado, June, 1970.

- Lay foundations for his conversion [life commitment] when he reaches accountability [responsible decision-making].
- Provide a foundation for his continuing growth and service as a Christian and a church member . . .[2]

Your first task as a teacher of children is to determine your own objective. This objective, of course, will be consistent with your church's goals and objectives. Determine your objective, and only after you have done this, be concerned with the "how" and the "when" of reaching that objective. In too many church situations people are conscientiously teaching who are more concerned with the *how* to teach than they are with *what* they are teaching.

To determine a sound objective calls for a mature theology. As a teacher you must know what you believe about the great biblical doctrines before you can effectively teach children the basic concepts about these doctrines.

Three basic ingredients of Christian education are the Learner (pupil), the Teacher, the Curriculum.

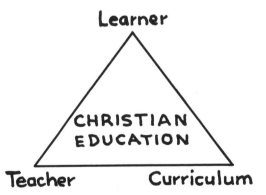

These three must be fused into one, and yet each one must play its distinctive role. The objectives and principles of Christian education given on the preceding and following pages speak to the sum total of these three elements. Let's look at each one separately and the distinctive role that each plays in the overall program of Christian education.

---

[2] Eugene Chamberlain, Robert A. Harty, Saxe Adams, *Preschoolers at Church* (Nashville: Convention Press, 1969), pp. 3–4. Used by permission.

The Learner (pupil)

The very object of Christian education centers on the learner, and in the context of this book, the learners are the boys and girls of elementary school age. The learner becomes the target of our efforts. Our prayers, planning, and teaching are all focused on the learner— the child.

This learner—what he is like, what he can do, what he can't do— will greatly determine the way we teach him. How ridiculous it would be to engage the pupil in work he can't understand or in a job that requires skills he doesn't possess. Before we can teach, we must know our children.

First of all, we must know the range of abilities that are normal for children this age. Time will be well spent studying materials on human growth and development of the elementary age child. There are a number of good books available on this subject.[3]

But that isn't enough. We must know the individual boys and girls that we teach. For instance, if Lane is a poor reader, we won't embarrass him each week by asking him to read aloud. If Susan is artis-

---

[3] Marjorie Stith, *Understanding Children* (Nashville: Convention Press, 1969).

tic, she can be given opportunity to participate in projects requiring this talent. Kevin, whose father is dead, needs a father (male) substitute. Knowing this, Mr. Frazier plans weekday contacts with Kevin. The learner's needs and abilities determine our teaching approaches in Christian education.

The child (the learner) must be the focus of the triangle in Christian education. When the teacher forgets his target, his work and planning are done in vain. Look at the child you teach and see what he is like. How can he be motivated? What interests him and what are his abilities? Capitalize on these as units of study are planned. Involve him in projects geared to his interest. Let him experience rather than just hear. Remember the experiences of this year will not necessarily be desirable for next year's girls and boys. Each group is unique with interests different from other groups.

The Teacher

The second part of the important triangle in church education is the teacher. The teacher will determine to a large degree the Christian education boys and girls receive. This responsibility is awesome for many of the children you teach will be from spiritually impoverished homes. Their knowledge of God and response to him will be determined by your teaching and living.

As a Christian teacher of children, you can identify with Moses' mother when Pharaoh's daughter said, "Take this child away, and nurse him for me, and I will give you your wages" (Ex. 2:9, RSV). The church has said to workers with children, "Take these boys and girls and teach them—teach them in a way that will eventually result in changed lives, as they encounter Jesus."

As important as nice buildings and good curriculum materials are, these are secondary to good teachers. An effective teacher can provide good learning experiences without buildings or curriculum materials. Teachers of children must possess the ability to communicate with boys and girls—communicate with a love that speaks of genuine interest in the individual. Not all adults have this ability. In James 3:1 (RSV) we read, "Let not many of you become teachers, my brethren, for you know that we who teach shall be judged with greater strictness."

The Curriculum

There are many definitions from the field of education for curriculum. Some define curriculum as the sum total of all learning experiences resulting from a planned course of action while others suggest that curriculum is merely the plan suggested to be followed by the workers. Colson and Rigdon in *Understanding Your Church's Curriculum* gave a very adequate definition in saying: "A church's curriculum may be thought of as the sum of all learning experiences resulting from a curriculum plan used under church guidance and directed toward attaining a church's objective." [4]

We are concerned that the curriculum afford children the kinds of learning experiences consistent with the church's objectives for Christian education.

Care should be taken that curriculum materials for Christian education are centered on the Bible. The degree and complexity of the content will be determined by the ages and development of the learners. For instance the first grader because of his limited ability and skill should be limited to sections of the Bible more easily understood. On the other hand, the sixth grader will be able to comprehend

---

[4] Howard P. Colson, Raymond M. Rigdon, *Understanding Your Church's Curriculum* (Nashville: Broadman Press, 1969), p. 38.

much more of the biblical revelation than a first grader will be able to comprehend.

Some questions that you as an educator should ask concerning your curriculum materials are:

1. Are they biblically sound?
2. Are they doctrinally accurate?
3. Are sound educational approaches employed?
4. Are the understanding level and skill development of the learner not violated?
5. Does the curriculum plan center on the learner rather than the teacher?
6. Does the curriculum plan seek to involve the learner at all levels?

A good curriculum seeks to involve the learner in discovering, exploring, evaluating, and appropriating. Quite often a teacher stops at the discovering or exploring level and therefore the job is only half done. Boys and girls must be lead to discover and explore the message in the Bible; however, they must be carried further if the biblical message is to be relevant. After discovering what the message is, they must evaluate this message in light of their own personal needs. As they appropriate the message, it actually becomes a part of their life. This becomes the real test in teaching.

Fourth-grade Jimmy had been involved in a mission study in which Eskimo customs, food, and dress were the subjects for several projects. Toward the end of the study, Johnny was asked what an igloo was. His response was that it was a round white thing made of papier-mâché and put on a cardboard. He had missed completely the purpose of the study to learn how Eskimos live.

In most public schools boys and girls are taught to explore and investigate, to do research, to listen to tapes, to use multi-media in the learning process. The strong implication is that no one person (teacher) can know all the information that needs to be learned. Therefore, the teacher becomes a learner along with the children. The teacher guides the boys and girls in using resource materials and this search becomes the core of the learning process. This involvement causes learning to be interesting and exciting, not just listening and trying to memorize. Rather than just hearing, the children are experiencing. The diagram of this sort of teaching/learning process looks like that shown on the following page.

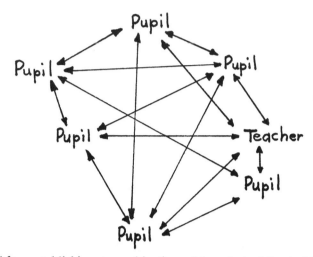

After establishing your objective—"the what of the task"—you need some guiding principles. The following are given as guideposts in teaching children. As you read these and ponder their meaning, hopefully you will see them as commonsense rules. By observing these principles, you will be less concerned with methodology. If you find a method of teaching where these principles cannot be used, the method is probably faulty or undesirable. Principles should, therefore, determine methodology. Underlying these principles is the biblical concept, namely, the worth of the individual.

The principles are grouped in four main areas: personal development, spiritual development, leadership, and approaches to teaching. The first two areas relate to the child, while the last two center on the worker.

Personal development (of the child)

1. *Respect each child as an individual and as a person of worth.*

As we take time to listen to Kim when she wants to tell us something, we are demonstrating to her that she is important, that what she has to say is worth listening to! Respect means accepting the ideas of children as well as adults. One teacher practicing this principle was heard to say, "I'm sorry Beth, you were right and I was wrong. Let's follow your idea which is a good one!" Any worker who says anything to a child that he would be embarrassed to say to an adult probably isn't respecting the child as a person of worth.

The way we act toward the child reflects respect (or the lack of it).

2. *Help the child think for himself.*

Good teaching constantly stimulates thinking, both from the learner and the teacher. True Christian education must produce good thinkers. If teaching doesn't stimulate thinking, has one really taught? God has created individuals with the ability to think and make decisions, and this ability needs developing. Questions that can be answered merely by a yes or no or a nod of the head are poor questions and stimulate little or no thinking. Try questions that require real thought, and watch children thrive on the challenge.

Before a child can make a meaningful life commitment, he must do *much* thinking. Therefore, as we help him think for himself, we are actually laying a foundation for his life commitment to God through Jesus Christ. Let's prepare him for that!

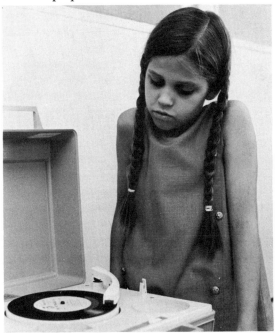

3. *Give the child opportunities to make decisions.*

Life is filled with decisions. Teaching should equip the child to make decisions wisely. Just how is this accomplished? First, we need to offer many opportunities for boys and girls to make little decisions

—decisions they can adequately and intelligently make. In the teaching/learning situation, let them decide how to make the map scene. Let Joey decide if the puppets should be made of balloons or paper bags. Let Kim decide whether to use red or green paint on the mural. Later in life, Kim and Joey will have to make decisions of all kinds and will require many skills in decision-making. Opportunities to make many decisions now—geared to their development and ability —will aid them throughout life.

Sooner or later in life, Kim and Joey will have to decide about life commitment to God. Helping them learn to make intelligent decisions will equip them and lay foundations for this most important decision in life.

4. Provide opportunities for each child to express himself.

Creativity is the spark that can make life interesting and exciting. God made each boy and girl different from any other boy or girl in the whole world. Therefore we should not expect the same behavior or expressions from each child. Today's educational scene offers many materials and methods through which the Christian message can be expressed. Consider these materials and methods and determine to provide many ways for your boys and girls to express themselves.

Self-expression isn't limited to materials. Consider Sally who talks incessantly. This is her way of expression, while Lisa expresses herself artistically. Beth's mode of expression may be writing, while Jerry's is music. Teaching approaches should provide all of these as avenues of learning as well as means of expression.

When a variety of methods and materials are offered, each child can more nearly find his niche and express himself adequately.

5. *Use a positive approach with firmness.*

Discipline will not become a problem when boundaries are well defined and a firm positive approach is used by the teacher. Boys and girls of elementary school age have been known to successfully scare away an adult teacher! Such fright usually occurs because the teacher is unsure of himself, has made inadequate preparation, or fails to be firm. Firmness does not mean coldness or unfriendliness. Be firm with a smile!

Most suggestions can be made to boys and girls in a positive rather than a negative way. We all respond to a positive suggestion better than to a negative statement. Practice turning your negative statements into positive ones. For example: "We walk in the room" rather than "Don't run in the room." "Let me show you a better way to carry the chair" instead of "Don't carry the chair on top of your head!" Some statements or signs provoke the opposite of the desired result. For example, what do you usually do when you see a sign that says "Wet Paint" or when you drive through a tunnel where a sign is posted "No horn blowing." The negative approach often brings the undesirable response.

6. *Be consistent in all relationships with the child.*

There is a great need for each worker to be consistent in all his work with children. The age and society in which we live is changing. In all this change, boys and girls want people who are stable to whom they can relate. Each teaching situation creates a need for rules, but keep these to a minimum. However, when a rule is made, stick with it. Be consistent!

7. *Encourage each child to finish the work he has begun.*

In churches today there are too many adults who did not learn this principle, or at any rate they are not applying it. In teaching/learning situations, give opportunity for choices and decisions to be made by the learner; but when Susan chooses a task, help her stay with it until completion. A real sense of accomplishment comes to the person who completes a job. When a child is permitted to choose and select, but then fails to finish a task, he is learning that it is all right to go through life accepting responsibility and then walking off and leaving it unfinished. Care should be taken to prevent children from choosing jobs too difficult, that require undeveloped skills. Beth Anne, a beginning reader, wants to work on a project that requires research. The skilful teacher will assist Beth Anne to make another choice of a project that is within her range of learning skills and abilities.

8. *Sincerely compliment the child.* Almost every person is seeking approval from those about him. This is especially true of the boys and girls we teach. It really takes a very mature person—even for an adult—to be unaffected by the disapproval of his peers. As desirable behavior patterns are practiced, reward them with a compliment. How much better it is to compliment than to correct. A compliment directed toward Jerry, Joe, and Derek will cause on-looking Craig to imitate their behavior because he, too, wants approval of his teacher.

Compliments should always be sincere. Compliment actions or behavior pattern rather than things. "Joe, you have worked hard on the rebus. Thank you for doing a good job." You are complimenting the process rather than the product.

9. *Be alert to the needs of each child in the room.*

We do not teach "lessons" nor do we teach classes or departments —we teach individuals. For teaching to be effective, it must be tempered by a recognition of individual needs and a plan to meet these needs in a teaching/learning situation. Nor can we look for an "average" and plan our teaching for the average—that approach will probably hit no one! A great deal is being said today about individualized instruction—or a teaching plan geared to each pupil's needs, allowing progress at his own rate of work and growth. Regardless of how far we go in this approach, we must think of Jill, Karen, Betty, and Jeff as we plan and as we teach. Karen's interest and ability in art will probably remind us to use this medium with her in teaching biblical concepts. Jill's musical ability can be utilized to learn other concepts related to the unit. Know that Jeff, a fourth grader, has an IQ of 130 tells us enrichment materials will be needed and essential if he is to be challenged during the unit. On and on the list will go until each child's needs have been considered.

Spiritual Development

Because each child is different and his rate of development varies from others, it is impossible to say that at a given age every boy or girl will have grasped a certain theological concept. An idea understood by one child at age seven may still be too difficult for another child at eleven. Previous experiences, learning abilities, and mental development all help determine the child's ability to grasp concepts. Beth who has a wonderful relationship with her father and loves him devotedly, gets one picture of God when the teacher refers to God as a father; yet Timothy who lives with his mother and has no father nor a close relationship with a Christian man gets an entirely different concept of God when the teacher refers to God as a father. Sometimes we forget that concepts must be based on experiences as well as knowledge.

Six-year-old Todd said to his three-year-old sister, "Lisa, when you talk to God, you don't have to say thank you for God and Jesus both—they are the same!" The three-year-old looked questioningly at her brother, then asked, "Are they twins?" His quick reply was, "No, they are just the same." Lisa then looked away and said, "Well, if they aren't twins, they couldn't be the same."

Here a very difficult and highly abstract concept was beginning to emerge for Todd. It was far too difficult for Lisa, so she dismissed it. The closest thing in her experiences to this was twins, and when she found out it wasn't twins, she quit trying to understand what Todd meant.

The following principles can serve as guidelines for helping children in their spiritual development.

1. *In conversation and prayer, use language the child understands, avoiding symbolism as much as possible.*

Boys and girls of the elementary school age are in a stage of transition. As a preschooler, the child experiences difficulty with concepts such as time, relationships, and other abstract ideas. As he enters school, he begins dealing with symbols (alphabet, numbers) and yet he often gropes for understanding when abstract ideas are thrown at him.

How much better it is for us to use Bible stories, missions stories, Bible verses, and child-experience stories that have meaning for children than to use those steeped in symbolism. Later in his growth and development he will learn that Jesus is the "light of the world." But now let's dwell on such concepts as "Jesus is my best friend." The Good Shepherd will have little meaning to a child who has neither seen a shepherd nor understands the shepherd's relationship to his sheep. But he can learn that God loves and takes care of us.

Knowledge and experience must merge if there is to be understanding. Teaching without understanding is of little value. Conversation and prayer should be experienced by the boys and girls on their level.

A first grader while hiking with her parents approached the crest of the mountain. As the panoramic scene of many miles came into view, this child spontaneously burst forth into song:

God's beautiful world,
God's beautiful world,
I love God's beautiful world.
He made it for me,
He made it for you,
I love God's beautiful world.

AURORA M. SHUMATE

In adult language, the child was relating the biblical concept of God as creator to her everyday experiences. This response did not have to be prompted by a teacher, but came spontaneously. Such experiences as this assure that desirable concepts have become a part of the child.

The spiritual development that is so very important is often times caught rather than taught. The capacity to infect others with one's own ideas and beliefs is a quality that must be a part of the teacher's life and personality. Without realizing it, he is teaching moral and spiritual values.

2. *Use Bible verses naturally in storytelling and conversation.*

Through Bible verses, God's plan can be conveyed to girls and boys by informal conversation and learning games. Quite often a Christian concept is embodied in a Bible verse. Relating these Bible verses to everyday life reinforces the total approach to Christian education. In order for a teacher to do this effectively, he must know many Bible verses. These verses need to be carefully selected with the capacities of the learner in mind. (The appendix has a number of Bible verses listed under subject areas. These have been carefully selected with the child, grades 1–6 in mind. These verses will supplement those suggested in your curriculum materials.)

One of the most popular ways to teach Bible verses to boys and girls is through learning games. These games may be in the form of a crossword puzzle, creative writing, ticktacktoe, or others. A sample of this type learning game is a "Match the Letter" game. If the purpose is to help boys and girls learn five Bible verses, prepare ten cards. On one side of the cards print the first ten letters of the alphabet. On the backs, print the first half of the Bible verse on one card and the second half on another card. In playing the game, the pupil will call two letters; turn these two over to see if the two parts match. Each one playing takes a turn until verses are matched correctly. With guidance, not only are the verses learned, but concepts are discussed.

3. *Refer to the Bible in problem-solving situations.*

One of the great needs in Christian education is to help boys and girls relate the Bible to the everyday problems of life. It is interesting to watch the reaction of a group that discovers our laws and judicial systems are based on the Ten Commandments. The biblical concept of ministry or helping those in need takes on new meaning as the pupil is led to actually participate in a ministry project.

For this reason boys and girls need to be led to see that the Bible is not just isolated, unrelated episodes but that the Bible is one continuous story of how God has shown himself to man. The older elementary age child can begin to develop a consciousness about history and historical events. He can get some idea of sequence and cause and effect. Exploring this message in the Bible, he is beginning to realize the consequences or penalty of not following God's laws.

4. *Provide many opportunities for children to grow in their concept of prayer.*

The child's concept of God (or Jesus) will greatly determine his attitude toward prayer. These concepts, feelings, or attitudes will be colored far more by praying persons with whom he comes in contact than it will by being told stories or facts about prayer. The worker who prays to God in a relaxed and communicative way in the presence of children is teaching boys and girls that God is near, that God hears us and answers our prayers in a way that is best for us. The teacher who prays in a tone other than his natural voice may be teaching boys and girls that to pray you must first learn to talk a special way. Workers will use a vocabulary that has meaning to the child. Some simple and yet significant things to keep in mind concerning prayer as you teach children are:

(1) *We can pray to God at any time and in any place.*

Therefore avoid having a prayer period at only one specified time during each teaching session. Look for a time when prayer can be spontaneous, a time when true gratefulness can be expressed. One second grader looking at a picture of Mary, Joseph, and baby Jesus began softly singing a Christmas song. This was followed by a worker nearby saying, "Let's thank God for Christmas and sending Jesus." The two bowed their heads and experienced true worship. Care should be taken to help boys and girls know that prayer isn't limited to the church building. Thanking God for food at mealtime helps the child relate prayer to everyday life.

(2) *Refrain from having children memorize prayers or from using memorized prayers.*

A memorized prayer quite often becomes a crutch that prevents one from having genuine prayer experiences. Perhaps the easiest place for one to fall into this trap is with the blessing said prior to eating our meals. One (child or adult) can recite some memorized prayer and never feel the emotion of gratefulness or worship. How refreshing it is to hear the preschooler say "Thank you God for the peas, potatoes, and meat. Amen."

In preparing for a prayer experience in church, rather than always saying, "Now let's pray," try, "Let's talk to God at this time. We'll bow our heads and close our eyes and think about all God does for us. Some of you may want to talk to God outloud while others pray silently. God hears all of us when we talk to him."

(3) *We can talk to God in any position.*

Because prayer is related to all facets of life, let's not limit it to only one corner or area. Avoid asking the child to always get in the same position to pray whether this position is standing, kneeling, or sitting. He may get the idea that for him to pray he must assume that position. Avoid requiring the child to do anything that is unnecessary in regard to prayer.

For instance, asking a child to fold his hands to pray is merely teaching him to do something that he later will probably unlearn. Folded hands don't induce a more reverent atmosphere.

The writer made the mistake of telling a group of third graders that we always bow our heads and close our eyes to pray. Eight-year-old Steve said, "Well, the preacher doesn't bow his head or close his eyes when he prays. He looks up!" After observing the pastor that Sunday, I had to agree with Steve!

Workers who feel the personal need for prayer will teach boys and girls the necessity of a growing prayer life. These attitudes and feelings of the workers are sensed by children. These things that are important to the workers become important to the boys and girls. In a real sense these attitudes and behavior patterns are caught rather than taught.

(4) *When children use the "language of Zion," don't be fooled into thinking they grasp more than they do.*

There are many words and phrases in the Christian religion that have meaning to adults. Children soon learn to use these phrases but many have no understanding of their meaning. A child who parrots these well-worn phrases can easily do so without understanding the significance or meaning. However, when Jeff puts these ideas into his own words and can verbalize the concept without using these well-worn phrases, the worker can then determine if the biblical concept is being understood.

Leadership

Even though an entire chapter will be devoted to the teacher as a key factor in learning, the following principles will provide a framework on leadership for the book. No teaching situation will be any stronger than its weakest teacher. Leadership will set the pace and determine goals for the teaching situation. The value of a strong and committed leadership cannot be overemphasized. These principles and techniques are:

1. *Workers using soft voices in the room will help set a climate for a relaxed learning situation.*

Individuals react spontaneously to sound. A loud sudden noise is annoying; soft music is relaxing. People eating when music with a rapid beat is played eat faster than those eating by soft music with a slower beat.

Likewise, the noise factors in a room affect the learning atmosphere. Some noises cannot be controlled, but let's begin with those that can be—the worker's voices. Quite often boys and girls who talk loudly are only following the example of their teacher(s). When you talk to a child, deliberately lower your voice and see his reaction. His reply will usually be the same soft one you used. What a quieting effect this can have on an entire room of twenty-five boys and girls. Remember, your voice becomes the thermostat!

Miss Duncan, a new public-school teacher of first graders, related a noise problem she was having with her children. This continued

through her first several weeks of school until she went to school one morning with laryngitis. Suddenly she discovered the solution to her noise problem. That day she had to whisper and all twenty-one first graders whispered.

2. *Visiting among workers is discouraged while in the department teaching children.*

If individual needs are being met as boys and girls are taught, there is no time for teachers to visit with each other during the teaching session. Of course, there will be normal communication necessary for good teaching/learning but workers should refrain from getting together to "just talk or visit" during the teaching session.

3. *Planning is essential if maximum learning takes place for the child.*

Later in the book an entire chapter will be devoted to the planning process; however, no set of principles for leadership could be given here and omit planning. Planning is so much a part of good teaching that you cannot have one without the other. No worker who is unwilling to plan, both individually and with the team of teachers, should accept a teaching assignment in his church.

4. *We do not have to talk to the child for him to learn.*

With so much emphasis being given to individualized instruction and to programed learning, we are reminded anew of this important principle. For many years in our churches, we felt that in order to teach Johnny, we had to "tell him what he should know." The real truth of the matter was that the one who was *really* doing the learning was the teacher and not Johnny. Telling a child a fact doesn't guarantee that he has learned that fact.

However, aside from individualized instruction and programed learning, boys and girls learn much from their workers that isn't verbalized. For instance, the teacher who comes regularly to teach boys and girls at church but who does not stay for the corporate worship is really teaching that the worship services of the church are unimportant and do not warrant our attendance and participation.

Boys and girls learn much from each other, and our teaching situation should provide opportunity for interchange of ideas and discussion in the learning sessions. Quite often a truth or an idea will be discovered by fifth-grade Jerry, and he states this truth in such a way that others in the group immediately grasp the truth.

5. *Avoid showing favoritism to one or more pupils.*

Any thoughtful teacher will immediately see the dangers in showing favoritism to individuals in the group. Children are quick to sense this and usually react negatively to it. It is true there are boys and girls in almost any group toward which you may be drawn. However, the quiet or the withdrawn boy is probably the one who needs your love and attention more than the outgoing child to whom you feel drawn.

6. *Workers teach more through their "lives" than through their words.*

This principle is closely related to number 4 in this grouping, and yet there is so much truth in it that it needs to be stated separately. Teachers of elementary age children become dominant figures in the lives of these children. This is true not only in the classroom but wherever the child sees the worker. The supermarket, the shopping center, the recreation park are some of the places where contact is made. Words, attitudes, behavior patterns that violate teachings away from the church usually nullify those teachings at church. For instance, if Mr. Jones has tried in the church setting to convey the idea of honesty and yet Jerry sees him accepting incorrect change at the supermarket, Jerry will probably accept the latter as the "lesson taught."

Five-year-old Beth attended kindergarten where much was said about thanking God for the food he gives us. Each day the boys and girls were led to say thank you to God for the snack. Later in the year while eating out with her parents, Beth saw Miss Bradford, her kindergarten teacher, who was also eating in the same cafeteria. They exchanged greetings and went to their separate tables. The next day at kindergarten, Miss Bradford was greeted by Beth who said, "I saw you yesterday at the cafeteria" to which Miss Bradford said, "Yes, Beth, I saw you. Did you have a nice dinner?" Then quite seriously Beth said, "I thought you told us to always thank God for our food." the teacher replied, "Yes, Beth I did. Didn't you see me bow my head?" Beth answered, "Yes, Miss Bradford, I saw you bow your head, but your lips didn't say anything!"

Children are far more observant than adults which compels us to live lives consistent with the words we teach.

Approaches to Teaching

The purpose of this book is not to get into the area of methodology but more the "why" of our teaching girls and boys in a church setting. Yet there are principles that guide us in using methods effectively in church. There are a number of good books that go into the details of methods or that give a listing of various methods appropriate to use with boys and girls. One such book is *Guiding Children* by Rives and Sharp.[5]

1. *Because children differ in interest and abilities, we give them many different approaches and opportunities to develop the project or activity on which they work.*

Even in smaller teaching situations with three or four boys and girls, more than one method, project, or activity should be used. Children are different and are interested in different things. For this reason, we give the choices and offer them opportunities in planning ways the project will be developed. For after all, the only reason to have an activity or project is to teach a truth or biblical concept. The project or activity becomes the avenue through which we teach. It guarantees participation by the learner which is essential. This involvement of the learner shifts from a teacher-centered approach to a pupil-centered approach.

2. *In using different media of art work, simple rules should be made and observed.*

The large array of art media provides many opportunities for teaching boys and girls biblical or other concepts. It is one thing to talk about the towns of Capernaum, Nazareth, and Jerusalem, but the relationship of these towns to one another will be much clearer if the group takes art materials and makes a map locating them and showing the distances between each. One group of fifth graders in studying a unit on the life of Peter, made a mural of Capernaum and the Sea of Galilee. In order to draw this picture, the group had to do research and learn that there were hills on which this town was located on the shore of the sea. They had to learn about the kind of houses people lived in during this period. What kind of trees and vegetation were around? Before the mural was completed, the boys felt almost at home as this little Galilean seaport was discussed.

A variety of art materials should be kept on hand and made accessible to the boys and girls for their use. This will necessitate some

---

[5] Elsie Rives, Margaret Sharp, *Guiding Children* (Nashville: Convention Press, 1969).

simple rules to follow to protect furnishings and clothing. When accidents do occur, those involved clean up the mess. Protective smocks can be used with such media as tempera paint or colored chalk. The following materials are inexpensive and could be kept on hand for use in teaching projects or activities:

felt-tip pens, tempera paint (powdered tempera to which water is added is less expensive), paint brushes, newsprint, table paper (rolls 36–42 in. wide) newspaper, cloth for costumes, posterboard, scissors, glue, crayons, masking tape.

3. *In using art work with boys and girls, avoid the use of "patterns" because they limit the child's creative ability.*

In all of our teaching we want to use methods which will require the learner to think and to create. The use of patterns prevents this. If in studying the customs of Jewish dress a teacher gives the pupil a picture (pattern) already drawn, the only thought processes the pupil has to experience is "what color do I paint each piece of the garment?" However, the effective teacher will lead the group to do research on the types of clothes and then have the group to draw, paint, or even make the garments. Patterns tend to make everything alike which is just the opposite of the way God has created us. There are no two persons alike, and each of us has his unique way of expressing himself. Perhaps one reason many churches are ineffective today results from the "pattern approach."

4. *Cooperative team work should result from activity or project experiences.*

One of the purposes of Christian education is to equip our children and youth to participate in effective team work. Learning to work together is one of the biggest and most difficult jobs most people have to learn. Yet to accomplish the basic mission of the church requires team work. No church can fulfil its mission with individuals working independently and each going his own way.

In teaching children, we can begin laying foundations for this type of work through the use of projects or activities. Small groups work together on a project designed to guarantee learning in specified content areas. This cooperative effort begins when the unit is introduced and the boys and girls become involved in the planning process. The projects then become pupil centered and not teacher centered even though the teacher guides the group. Choices are given to involve the learners in all phases of the development. Each pupil can make his contribution according to his readiness and ability. The group (pupils) decide the process through which the project will emerge—a basic skill to fruitful Christian living is being learned.

Occasionally a worker may forget the purpose of an activity or project and become more concerned with the finished product than the process. The learning takes place during the process and therefore the workers greater concern will be with the process. Once a Palestinean village is made, dispose of the project and move on to another learning experience. The learning of Palestinean customs, food, dress, homes, and so forth will take place as the village is being made. Questions are asked, answers sought, research done, meaningful learning conversation engaged in. This is the learning process. Once the model village is completed, it can be shared with the larger group and the information learned shared with others in the room. At this point the project has served its purpose. It should be taken out of the room and disposed of at the discretion of the teacher and/or group. Having it around the next year may prevent another group from engaging in this type of learning. A group the following year in learning about Palestinean customs may participate in making a mural or collage.

5. *Workers do not "touch up" work done by the child.*

The worker who feels it is necessary to "touch up" art work of children has lost sight of the purpose of the art work. Caution should be taken when the group has an "open house" or puts their work on display that time isn't spent on projects just to show off and not teach. The main purpose is teaching, and every minute of the time we have should be spent in teaching.

With the preceding principles in mind, it is hoped that the teacher will develop his own philosophy of and approach to teaching boys and girls in a church setting.

CHAPTER TWO
"TEACHING
WITH DIMENSION"

Teaching is
—listening to a child who has a problem.
—being late to the session.
—saying, "Thank you, Karen, I'm glad you are my friend."
—showing an attitude of "I don't care."
—refusing to be tolerant of others who are different.
—caring enough to visit in Barry's home.
—looking disapprovingly at Beverly who spills the paint.
—referring to the Bible in problem-solving situations.
—being well prepared.

To some people, teaching is conveying facts to a group of pupils. To some others, it is merely "keeping a group." However, as the above statements indicate, teaching is a way of life! We are constantly teaching by the way we respond to Henry's question, by the way we react when an announcement is made to our group, even by the way we walk across the room.

Mrs. Haynes was directing a large-group learning experience while at a most inopportune time, Mrs. Case entered the room, interrupted the session to make what seemingly was an insignificant announcement. The expression of disgust on Mrs. Hayne's face was soon mirrored on the faces of several first graders in the room. Teaching was taking place even without verbal communication.

What is your definition of teaching? How would you define the concept? Hopefully this book will provide some avenues through which teaching can become an exciting adventure—not only for the pupil but also for the teacher. When we teach with dimension, desirable learning does take place.

Have you ever stopped to consider how boys and girls view teaching? The quotes on the following page are from boys and girls of elementary age:

In reporting on a research project conducted in a school in Selah, Washington, Kellman describes the transition in this primary school from the traditional subject-matter approach to the approach where there are areas of interest in which each child can explore, investigate, and participate in learning tasks. He identified the two basic aims of this primary-school experience as (1) to develop a healthy self-image and (2) a reading ability at grade level or better. Following this report, Kellman concludes by saying, "This group of teachers is now thoroughly convinced that the role of the teacher is no longer that of the traditional 'subject matter expert.' The role of the modern teacher is that of learning experience creator —one who creates relevant learning situations that are important and meaningful to students." [1]

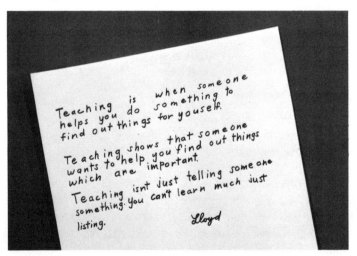

Perhaps one of the best definitions of teaching comes from the Bible. "But every one when he is fully taught will be like his teacher." (Luke 6:40b, RSV). This is the genuine test of teaching with dimension—when lives are changed and molded toward a desirable model.

Suppose the three following episodes were taking place in the same department room. Each teacher on this team has a different concept of teaching. Look at each of the three episodes and then determine which teachers' concept is the one closest to teaching with dimension.

Mrs. Bension begins the small-group work by saying, "I'm sorry

---

[1] Clair M. Nicholson and Robert A. Kellman, "When Primary Children Do Their Own Thing." Unpublished report, July, 1970. Used by permission.

I was so late today. We overslept this morning and . . . Now let's see, is today the second Sunday of the unit? Did any of you study your lesson?"

At one side of the table Barry and Jeff are deeply engrossed in a conversation about a scout camping trip planned for Tuesday night.

"Mrs. Benson," replies Susan, "I thought it was the third session in the unit—that's the one I studied."

Mrs. Benson says, "Well, let's all open our Bibles to Luke 10:25–37. While you are looking that up, I'll go over to the supply cabinet and see if I can find some construction paper. Maybe we can write some words we don't understand from this Scripture passage.

In the same room, Mrs. Woods is working with her group of seven fourth graders. The project this group has planned is to research the synagogue schools in an attempt to gain a better understanding of the education Jesus received as a boy. On the table is a Bible atlas, a Bible dictionary, and some leaflets from a local Jewish synagogue. Deeply involved in the experiences she had the past week, Mrs. Woods is telling about her visit to the Jewish synagogue. She is crushed when Stephen says, "I wish I were in the drama project. They are having so much fun."

Mr. Reagon arrives first in the department today. He arranges the chairs in an informal circle since their project today doesn't require a table. Under each chair he tapes a slip of paper. Beside his chair he places a New Testament map showing Judea, Samaria, and Galilee. Also three different pictures of the good Samaritan are placed on chairs in the small group.

Todd and Marianne arrive first. After a cordial greeting, Mr. Reagon asks each to choose one of the following "early times" games:

(1) Read from a modern speech version of the Bible Luke 10:30–37 (the story of the good Samaritan).

(2) On the map trace the most direct route from Galilee to Judea.

Study one of the pictures and imagine the conversation that took place between the hurt man and the Samaritan on their way to the inn. Write a script to go with it

Soon all six of the fourth graders in the drama project are present. As the individuals finish the early time games, Mr. Reagon says, "You remember from our unit planning, we decided to dramatize today the parable Jesus told about the good Samaritan. Let's think about how these persons might have felt in addition to what they said. Look under your chair and you will find a slip of paper. On the paper is written the name of one of the persons in the story. Now that you have the paper and know which person you are to represent, this is what I want you to do. Listen carefully as I tell the story as it is written in Luke 10.

After I tell the story, I want each of you to tell the story only from the viewpoint of the person you have. For instance, the innkeeper will tell only the part of the story he saw happen and then how he might have felt about it.

Are there any questions? All right, listen carefully and then it will be your turn to share with the group.

Following the telling of the story, Mr. Reagon calls on Gary whose slip of paper said "innkeeper." Gary replies: "Well I was busy working inside the inn when I heard a loud knock at the door. Boy, was I surprised when I opened the door and saw a Samaritan helping a hurt Jew off his donkey. The Samaritan man seemed real kind and helped the hurt man inside my inn. The Samaritan gave me money for the night's lodging. He then told me to take good care of the hurt man and he would pay me more the next time he was through our village. I first wondered if his credit was good, but I figured if he would help a man he didn't even know, he would surely pay his debts."

Jimmy is seated next to Gary, so Mr. Reagon asks him to tell which character he has. Jimmy replies that his slip of paper says," "priest."

"All right, Jimmy," responds Mr. Reagon, "Tell us how you think the priest felt."

Jimmy begins by saying, "Well, it was one of those busy days at the synagogue for me. I was late leaving home that morning and on the way to the village, I saw something lying in the road. When I came nearer, I saw it was a man, maybe dead. But when I was closer, I saw him breathing. He probably had been robbed and the robbers might still have been around. The thought scared me. Then I remembered the meeting I was going to and hurried on so I wouldn't be late. I crossed the road so I wouldn't have to go too close to the hurt man. As I left him, I thought maybe I should have stopped and helped, but I went on."

After a brief pause, Mr. Reagon asks who wants to be next. Paul said, "Since I have the good Samaritian, let me! Well, I was riding down the road on my donkey and when I went around a curve, there beside the road was a hurt man. He had been beaten. I saw he was a Jew, but thought, He is still a person and he needs help. I put some oil on his bruises and then helped him up on the donkey. As soon as we got to the next village, we looked up the inn and there we put some more medicine on his wounds. I had a little extra money so I paid the innkeeper for the man's room. It always gives you a good feeling inside when you help someone!"

Now look back at these three episodes. What makes the third episode (Mr. Reagon's group) far more desirable? The clue is involvement. Each learner had to do more than just "sit still and listen." He was involved from the very beginning of the session. The approaches used by Mr. Reagon caused each learner to have to think, reconstruct mental images, and analyze feelings.

Episode number 1 (Mrs. Benson's group) is the typical picture of the worker whose teaching is mostly negative. She is negative because of a lack of commitment; being untrained, and possibly lacking in skill. The education that boys and girls get who are exposed to a teacher like this is far from the desirable Christian education discussed in Chapter 1.

How did you feel about the teacher in Episode number 2 (Mrs. Woods' group)? Here is an example of a teacher who takes her job seriously and really wants to lead girls and boys in learning experience. However, there is one vital missing ingredient—understanding of how children learn. She didn't know or remember that learning must involve the pupil. How much better it would have been if she had taken the group—or representatives from the group—with her to the synagogue. As it was, she was the one doing the learning and was merely relating her learning to the group—which isn't enough. We learn through experiencing and therefore pupils need to be actively involved in learning projects where they are "doing." Each learner must be involved and have learning experiences rather than just being told about them.

Now inventory your teaching approach. Which of the three episodes does your teaching most closely resemble? Which example would you like it to resemble?

The erronous concept held by many teachers who teach in a

church setting is that the learning should be teacher centered. This puts the teacher in the center of the learning process rather than the pupil. This concept suggests that the teacher is the source of authority and knowledge. In reality it says that growth will be limited mainly to the teacher and not the pupils! In diagram form, the concept looks like this:

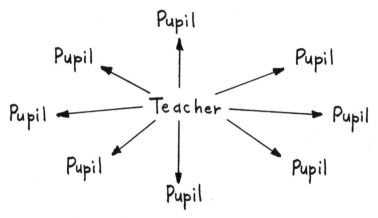

In fact, the potential involvement of this group allows for inter-action between all members of the learning group. To show this the diagram would have to show an arrow going from each person to all other persons in the group. You see immediately that the teacher is not the focal point, but still definitely guides the learning process. Usually the more involvement that can be brought about in the group will indicate the more potential learning.

If desirable teaching takes place, the pupil must utilize some thought processes. Only through participation and involvement of the pupil can we be insured that he is moving toward the desired outcomes for a unit of study. Unless we give him a chance to partici-pate verbally, he may look interested and may even be still and sit quietly; however, he may be thinking about what Mom will fix for dinner!

The test of our teaching comes when the learner must reconstruct thought patterns and ideas. We may spend five sessions on a unit on the life of Joseph (Gen. 37–47). If at the end, Jerry doesn't know the sequence of events in Joseph's life or how God worked through Joseph's life, we have failed in one level of teaching—because Jerry cannot reconstruct these events in his thinking. If our teaching doesn't give this opportunity for the boys and girls to be actively involved in reconstructing thought patterns and Bible stories/facts, potential learning is lost. This is why such methods as drama, questions and answers, recall, creative writing, art activities, and learning games are essential. They demand participation.

When developing a unit of study, your teaching plans should include a summary or review near the conclusion of the unit. This becomes a test of your teaching skill as well as a test of the learning that has taken place by the boys and girls. Summary and review will often clarify concepts for children. This activity may provide the repetition necessary for some to actually learn the facts or begin acquiring the concept.

One way to implement this idea of a summary or a post test is through learning games. An example is to play the learning game "Bible Ticktacktoe." Prepare a board or place four strips of masking tape on the floor to construct the framework for the game. On one stack of paper sheets, mark *O*'s on the front. On the other stack, mark *X*'s. On the back of each *X* or *O,* write a question based on the unit of study just concluding.

Divide the group into two parts and assign X's to one group and O's to the other group. (Or two children may play the game—one child taking the X's and the other child the O's). As each child takes one of the questions, he reads it aloud and if he can answer it correctly, he plays his X or O. If he doesn't know the answer, he forfeits a turn. This question that cannot be answered by the child is then dealt with in the large group and discussed. Hopefully the information will be clarified in the group discussion. Of course the first team getting three X's or three O's in a straight line wins the game. If additional questions are left, divide up and play the game again until all questions have been answered.

Suppose the unit had been on Joseph's life. Sample questions for the X's and the O's to play "Bible Ticktacktoe" could have been:

1. Who was Joseph's father?
2. Where did Joseph's family live?
3. How many brothers did Joseph have?
4. Tell about the problem Joseph had with his brothers?
5. Who was Joseph's grandfather?
6. Why didn't Joseph's brothers like him?
7. What evil did Joseph's brothers do to him?
8. What did Joseph do that got him out of prison?
9. Tell about the dreams of Pharaoh that bothered him.
10. What did Joseph do when he saw his brothers in Egypt?
1. Who was Joseph's Mother?
2. What did Joseph's family do to earn a living?
3. What kind of trip did Joseph's father send him on when he was a boy?
4. What promise did God make to Joseph's grandfather?
5. Was Joseph's family wealthy or not?
6. Tell about Joseph's trip to Egypt.
7. What did Joseph predict when he interpreted Pharaoh's dreams?
8. Why could Joseph interpret dreams?
9. Why did Joseph's brothers go to Egypt?
10. Name some ways God helped Joseph.

Determine now to teach with dimension. Good teaching includes planning for and securing involvement of the learner throughout the unit of study. A variety of methods will be employed that each pupil's interest will be gained.

This desirable teaching will move away from a lesson-to-lesson or meeting-to-meeting approach to the unit of study approach. Boys and girls will be actively involved from the beginning of the unit in the planning process. Thinking will be stimulated, involvement will be realized, Bible truths appropriated, and lives changed. When this happens, you are "teaching with dimension!"

I hear . . .
> I may remember

I see . . .
> I understand

I do . . .
> I know.

CHAPTER THREE
"BEING
ON THE TEAM"

"The tremendous explosion of human knowledge now in progress may shake the foundations of our society in the next twenty-five years. Will the churches be able to preserve human values?" writes D. Bruce Merrifield. He goes on to describe this age in which we live. "This is a most remarkable period in which we are living. The incredible explosion of human knowledge which has occurred in the last ten years will continue to rise . . . 90 percent of all the information ever developed in the physical and biological sciences has been developed only since 1940. All the Galileos, the Archimedes, the Newtons, and even the Einsteins have contributed less than 10 percent of our total knowledge in these areas. Moreover, it will double again in the next seven years and again after that in the following three or four years.[1]

Inference has already been made to the teaching approaches used in the public schools and the influence this has upon the church's teaching ministry. Those who teach in the church cannot escape the impact this revolution has on the boys and girls they teach. Because of the importance of Christian education, we will profit a great deal by constantly studying and evaluating teaching/learning approaches used in public schools. Only as we do this will we be able to adapt those suitable for Christian education.

Such has been the case with team teaching. In the middle 50's, the innovation of team teaching began to emerge in the public schools. In forecasting the impact of team teaching, Dr. James B. Conant says:

> There is without doubt a ferment among educators with respect to the conduct of elementary education. The long-standing notion of a self-contained classroom of thirty pupils taught by one teacher

---

[1] D. Bruce Merrified, "Tomorrow Is Unbelievable Today," *Baptist Program*. August, 1970, p. 10. Used by permission.

is giving way to alternative proposals. One of these proposals is team teaching, which, as we have seen, has advantages in orienting new teachers.

If the idea of team teaching becomes widely accepted—and many elementary school principals predict that it will—there will be places in classrooms for a wide range of instructional talent. How such schemes will work out over the years in practice remains to be seen, but team teaching seems to many the answer to the question of how to attract more of the ablest college students into elementary school teaching. The possibility of a teacher's having an opportunity to take advantage of her special field of interest is exciting.[2]

This idea of team teaching began to catch on in some religious denominations' Christian education program in the primary grades back as early as the middle 50's. However, only in recent years has it began to emerge in the elementary grades (4–7). The purpose of this chapter will be to explore the values of the team teaching approach as compared to assigning one teacher to one classroom of children for an entire year.

First of all let's examine some accepted definitions of team teaching from elementary education. "Team teaching is a type of instructional organization, involving teaching personnel and the students assigned to them in which two or more teachers are given responsibility, working together, for all or a significant part of the instruction of the same group of students." [3]

In the book *Team Teaching: Bold New Venture* Beggs defines team teaching as "an arrangement whereby two or more teachers, with or without teacher aides, cooperatively plan, instruct and evaluate one or more class groups in an appropriate instructional space and given length of time, so as to take advantage of the special competencies of the team members." He goes on to suggest that in public education there are many variations of this definition. This definition does suggest several major factors basic to any team plan such as:

cooperative planning, instruction, and evaluation

[2] James B. Conant, *The Education of American Teachers*. (New York: McGraw-Hill, 1963) p. 147. Used by permission from Educational Testing Service.

[3] Shaplin and Olds, editors, *Team Teaching*. (New York: Harper and Row, 1964), p. 15. Used by permission.

student grouping for special purposes (large group instruction, small group discussion [instruction], independent study)
flexible schedules
use of teacher aides
recognition and utilization of individual teacher talents
use of space and media appropriate to the purpose and content of instruction.[4]

Team teaching apparently has not only made an impact on public education, but has met with wide acceptance in a short period of time. A survey on team teaching was made in 1966 which reported that it becomes more common as the school system enrolment increases. It also revealed that about 1 in 10 of the small systems (enrolments of 300–2,999), 3 in 10 of the medium size systems (enrolments of 3,000–24,999) and 5 in 10 of the large systems (enrolments of 25,000 or more) used team arrangements for instruction in their elementary schools.[5]

What implications does team teaching in public education have for Christian education? It is not only difficult but impossible to take standards for public education and impose these on volunteer teachers in Christian education. Not only is there a difference between paid teachers and volunteer teachers, but also the content being taught is quite different. Much of the curriculum in Christian education centers in attitudes and behavior which go far beyond learning facts.

In discussing the advantages of team teaching in public education, Beggs lists some advantages that certainly apply to Christian education. The advantages applicable to both are:

1. The team approach offers the combined thinking of more than one person.

2. The team approach makes possible the "breaking in" of a neophyte [new recruit] teacher as beginning teachers can be teamed with experienced teachers.

3. The team makes it possible for more and better planning for the teaching of children.

4. The team enables each child to "sit at the feet" of both the

---

[4] *Team Teaching: Bold New Venture,* edited by David Beggs, III. Copyright © 1964 by Indiana University Press, p. 16. Used by permission of the publisher.

[5] National Education Association Bulletin (NEA Research Division, Washington, December, 1967). Used by permission.

good and the poor teacher. [In the usual Sunday School, the child is nearly always exposed to at least two teachers—one in the large group and one in the small group].[6]

Let's take the implications from team teaching in public education and adapt them wherever possible to enhance instruction in Christian education. Here is a church school situation in which the implications can be applied. In doing this, we will have a team of (volunteer) teachers numbering about four to six with a maximum enrollment of twenty-five boys and girls to each room. (maintaining a ratio of 1 teacher for every 7 pupils). These boys and girls can be adequately taught in one room approximately 24' by 32' (25 square feet per person). Of course, if few than twenty-five pupils are enrolled, the number of teachers will drop, maintaining the same ratio of one teacher for every seven pupils.

Of course many organizational patterns are referred to as "team teaching" both in public education and Christian education. In public education, teachers often specialize in a subject area and become the "expert" and lead teacher for that particular subject. For example, in the elementary grades one teacher may have responsibility for math while another person teaches in the area of language arts. A third teacher may join the team as the specialist in science. Because of professional training, skills, and even lack of funds, each teacher will teach several groups of children during the day in several rooms or the children will come to his room in several shifts.

However, in Christian education, this concept of team teaching breaks down. The team of two to four teachers is assigned to one classroom for the year. The teachers do not specialize in subject areas but each brings his particular knowledge and skills to the teaching setting and has responsibility in this one room for either a small group (up to 7 or 8) or the large group (up to 25). These teachers in the church setting become a team in teaching the same subject area. The team approach does allow the children to explore the subject area through several different approaches. In Chapter 5 this concept will be illustrated.

In many churches the traditional approach of one teacher assigned to one classroom of children for the entire year has been used. Sometimes the teaching approaches have been further weakened by

---

[6] Beggs, *op. cit.*

segmenting the schedule with an "opening exercise" which was not related to the curriculum content for the day or unit. In shifting away from this segmented approach of nonrelated material some Christian educators have coined the descriptive phrase of "total-period teaching." This, of course, is an underlying concept of team teaching. Regardless of the number of segments, groupings, or schedules, all of these parts must fit together toward some desired outcome. Therefore, the entire block or session becomes one teaching pattern with many integral parts.

When the traditional approach is used some weaknesses become apparent:

1. *Teaching becomes segmented with individual parts not fitting together.*—This is especially true when the group must relate to a large group unless the two teachers plan carefully together (becoming a team) working toward the same outcome. This is one of the biggest weaknesses of the traditional "opening assembly" or "closing assembly" when someone has been asked to bring a devotional thought. Large-group experiences need to lead directly into the small-group teaching, or if they come at the end, the large-group teaching experiences should undergird what has been taking place in the smaller groups. To bring this about, the two teachers must carefully plan together and insure that the large group (assembly) undergird and reinforce learning that was begun in the small group. This therefore becomes a "team teaching" approach.

2. *Group evaluation is lacking.*—To objectively evaluate one's efforts is an extremely difficult thing to do! When teachers are working by themselves in a self-contained classroom, the element of group evaluation is missing. This missing element becomes one of the greatest weaknesses in the traditional approach as opposed to team teaching. One teacher may be so close to a situation that he may not be able to see what is taking place. Or he may become so involved with one or two pupils that he misses some very important reactions from others in the group. When three or four teachers who work together sit down to evaluate, more accurate evaluation can take place.

3. *The group is deprived of the input of new ideas.*—When a teacher works alone in a classroom, he is deprived of the stimulation of new ideas from other teachers. A rich reward of team teaching is that opportunity of sharing ideas and of joint planning which results

in better teaching. Quite often in a planning meeting, Mr. Smith may suggest an idea. The idea has some merit but still needs refining. This idea sparks Mrs. Moore's thinking which she shares with group. Altering Mr. Smith's original plan a little, Mr. Best adds still another dimension. As a result, the team refines an idea and develops a good approach for teaching.

Quite often a teacher will say, "What I need is a shot in the arm." This "shot in the arm" comes regularly when a team of teachers work together in planning, teaching, and evaluating.

The organization of this team does require that one of the team members be assigned the responsibility for leading the other teachers as well as the boys and girls in the teaching/learning process. In a sense this teacher becomes the administrator for the group. He is often referred to as the "lead teacher," "director," "leader," or "superintendent." Usually it is his responsibility to lead the department not only in planning, instructing, and evaluating, but also in the large-group experiences (where all the small groups merge). Since this book deals mainly with the teaching aspect of Christian education rather than the administration of a program of Christian education, the term "lead teacher" will be used to designate this person.

The formation of small groups may vary from temporary groupings based on interest and skills to more permanent groupings based on developmental needs.

Some of the strengths of this variation of team teaching in Christian education are that each teacher on the team is

(1) Teaching toward the same desirable outcomes.

(2) Bringing his particular personality, skills, and background to the teaching setting (recognizing that his are different from the other team members).

(3) Reinforcing teaching done by the other teachers on the team.

In a leadership conference where this idea of team teaching was being presented and the relationship of the small groups to the large group was discussed, a conferee asked, "Just where is the lesson taught?" For a person not having used the team approach, this becomes a serious question. In the past, he has been totally responsible for the teaching. Now he must shift—still assuming responsibility but also sharing this responsibility. Therefore the answer becomes obvious—teaching takes place in both the small groups and the large group. In the vernacular of the question, "The lesson is taught during the entire session—in both small and large groups." Hopefully, what has been missed in the small group will be picked up in the large group and vice versa. Teachers join hands and commitment in teaching toward the desirable outcomes for each unit of study. Johnny may learn a concept while working on a map of the Bible lands in the small group. Seated beside him, Sammy worked on the same map but missed the concept; however, in large group as he viewed the filmstrip *The Land Where Jesus Lived,* Sammy caught the idea. And to Johnny the filmstrip in the large group reinforced the concept he began appropriating in the small group.

The lead teacher usually has responsibility for the large group and the unit of study is introduced in the large group at the beginning of the first session of the unit. In the following sessions, the large group will usually come at the end of the session; however, some sessions may be introduced with the large group or some session might even omit the large group. Flexibility is essential! The needs and progress of the pupils will determine schedules. Because schedules exist only for our purpose in teaching, we should not become slaves to schedules. A good curriculum plan will make suggestions about schedules, yet even there, flexibility must be maintained.

One of the more difficult aspects of team teaching is structuring the large group to insure its support of the work done in the small groups. The first step in accomplishing this is group planning. Each teaching member of the team must know what the others are doing. These parts (groups) must fit together in a total period of teaching. Therefore, the large group experience must be more than a devotional thought interspersed with songs, prayer, and announcements. Good curriculum plans will suggest possible avenues through which the content may be experienced. However, these methods exist only for the purpose of effectively conveying to the learner concepts, attitudes, or content and involving him to the degree that he begins appropriating them.

In planning for both the large and small groups, teachers will want to plan for worship experiences. Quite often these moments will come spontaneously for the children; however, planned worship should be a part of most large group experiences.

Assuming that the small groups have all been involved in projects or activities directly related to the desired outcomes of the unit of study, the lead teacher could choose one or more approaches from the following list in planning and developing the large group period. These approaches are types of large-group experiences which insure involvement and participation. It is the responsibility of the lead teacher to make sure large-group experiences are curriculum related.

1. *Sharing from small groups.*—Near the conclusion of a unit of study, this is a desirable technique that can be effectively used. Each group may have approached the unit through a different project or activity. The learning results from the activity of each group can be shared with the remaining groups, and thus all profit from the experiences. This sharing should be a natural outgrowth of the projects in which the group has been involved. The group sharing will remember that this is a time for sharing information learned and not a performance.

2. *Pretest and/or Post-test.*—Factual information on the unit can be tested prior to the unit or at the conclusion. If a pretest is used, the results should be shared with the teachers of the small groups. This information will greatly assist the teachers in planning the unit. The following is a sample of a test that could be given both at the beginning and at the conclusion of a unit on the life of Jesus.

THREE BUSY YEARS

How would you like to begin your study about Jesus by finding out how much you know about him now? Choose the answer you think is most nearly correct. Then at the end of the unit, you can take the test again and check your improvement.

1. (a) Solomon (b) Samuel (c) Isaiah prophesied about the coming Messiah.
2. (a) King David (b) Alexander the Great (c) Herod was king when Jesus was born.
3. Jesus was born in (a) 6 B.C. (b) A.D. (c) A.D. 6.
4. Mary and Joseph took Jesus to Egypt because of (a) his health (b) the king (c) Joseph's job.
5. When he was twelve, Jesus went to Jerusalem to (a) go to school (b) attend the Passover celebration (c) to see relatives.
6. Jesus was baptized by (a) John (b) Peter in (c) the Sea of Galilee (d) the Jordan River. (choose two)
7. Jesus had (a) 8 (b) 10 (c) 12 special helpers or disciples.
8. One of the disciples who wrote a book about Jesus was (a) Peter (b) Philip (c) John
9. Jesus raised (a) Zacchaeus (b) Lazarus (c) Simon from the dead.
10. Jesus' main enemies were (a) Pharisees (b) Roman soldiers (c) publicans
11. Just before he was arrested, Jesus prayed at (a) Capernaum (b) Mount Hebron (c) the garden of Gethsemene.
12. After the resurrection, Jesus was on earth (a) 15 days (b) 125 days (c) 40 days.

There are many variations to tests. If you are planning to give both a pretest and post-test, you may want to devise a post-test which covers the same material with different questions.

3. *Films and filmstrips.*—Many good films and filmstrips that can be used to undergird a unit are available on the market (both rental and purchase). Carefully preview the visual aid prior to the session to determine if it warrants showing. Prior to showing the film, orient

the group by asking them to look for specified things. Listening teams may be formed to report on assignments following the showing.

4. *Assignment and report.*—Assignments can be given by the lead teacher to various ones in the group. These assignments should usually be given at least a week in advance. A telephone call to remind the boys and girls is usually good precaution. Assign work that will supplement the unit of study. These assignments should be hard enough to challenge the age group and yet not too difficult for them to do. Observe the following assignments that were given to one group of fifth graders. Some are more difficult than others. There are some accurate statements and there are some with limiting concepts. Nevertheless, these provided the springboard for some healthy discussion involving most of the pupils in the large group. These assignments were given during a unit on Jesus:

—List the twelve disciples Jesus chose to be his "special helpers" and write a sentence about each one.

—Simon Peter grew up in what town? _____ Find out all you can about that town and then write a paragraph to share with the group next session.

—What was Simon Peter's occupation? _____ Find out all you can about this occupation and how it was done during the time Peter lived and then write a paragraph about it to share with the group next session.

—Find out at least five kinds of foods Simon Peter might have eaten during a meal. List these and if you can, bring some to show next session.

5. *Resource person.*—There are many units of study during which a resource person can profitably be used. This person may be on the church staff, a member of the church, a missionary, or a responsible person in the community. For instance, during a unit on the creation, a person who is trained and skilled in the area of ecology could make a valuable contribution in helping the boys and girls know how to preserve and want to care for the world God created for our use.

In one department, the group was studying about how God used Moses to give the children of Israel a code of laws (Ten Commandments). The lead teacher discovered that in the church membership was a man who had been to Egypt and had seen Mt. Sinai. A contact was made and a visit arranged. Faces of the girls and boys reflected excitement as they eagerly listened to the resource person who gave a vivid description of that part of the world. This description was then followed by the showing of slides he had taken. The resource person added a new dimension to the unit of study.

Before a resource person comes to the department, the lead teacher needs to:

(1) Clearly state the purpose he wants achieved through the visit of the resource person.

(2) Alert the resource person to areas of work already being done in the unit so as to avoid duplication.

(3) Establish time limitations for the resource person to work within.

(4) Create a relaxed climate for the resource person as he is introduced to the large group.

(5) Allow some time for questions and dialogue at the end.

Depending upon the nature of the study and the background of the resource person, time for the large group may need expanding when a highly qualified resource person is brought in.

6. *Map Study.*—Maps provide an intriguing study of far-away lands for boys and girls. Through the use of maps—both biblical and current—boys and girls are able to establish relationships to biblical history and current missions work.

A group of fifth graders were poring over a biblical map, determining the distance from Jerusalem to Bethany. Gary casually commented that his neighbor had just returned the day before from the Near East and had visited Jerusalem. Astonished Mike looked up and asked with almost disbelief, "You mean there is really a Jerusalem on this earth you can visit? Is it the same Jerusalem in the Bible?" A world of almost fantasy for Mike suddenly became one of reality because of map study!

In the large group, maps can be used to reinforce and verify study taking place in the small groups. The lead teacher may:

(1) Use a map on an overhead projector to trace a journey or identify specific locations. For instance, this would be an excellent preview or conclusion to a unit about the children of Israel making their exodus from Egypt to Canaan or to a unit tracing one of Paul's missionary journey's.

(2) On a large wall map, ask individuals to identify cities and countries being studied.

(3) Compare biblical maps to current-day maps. Acetate overlays are excellent for doing this if an overhead projector is available.

(4) Use a map setting to identify biblical customs, food, dress, and so forth.

7. *Displays.*—Boys and girls are natural "collectors." They enjoy helping build and develop a unit-related display. For example, during a unit on "The Bible, a Special Book," Carey brought the family Bible of several generations ago written in Dutch; Karen made tablets (using plaster of paris) to resemble those given to Moses. Susan brought a scroll that she had made with selected Old Testament Scripture passages written on it. Mark and Kevin worked during the week to complete a mezuzah and phylacteries. To this display workers added several translations and versions of the Bible. Bible study helps were also added.

In the large group, the lead teacher involved many of the boys and girls in relating these objects of the display to "The Bible, a Special Book." Heightened interest created an environment for learning through the display.

Displays are also very effective when the content of the unit centers on missionary education.

8. *Storytelling.*—Telling the Bible story or information related to the Bible story is one of the most popular approaches to the large group. This is especially true when the small groups in their projects or activities have not dealt specifically with the content of the Bible story for the given session. The use of the Bible story in the large group is more commonly employed for departments involving primary age children.

Of course storytelling in the large group isn't limited to Bible stories. There are many good missions stories and child-experience stories that convey biblical truths.

An open-end story provides opportunity for large group involvement. In this type story, the teacher creates the setting and leads the group up to the point of action. Here he stops and gives pupils the opportunity of finishing the story. This can be done orally or in written form. Take two or three of the endings prepared by the pupils and let the large group evaluate them.

Regardless of the type story being told, the lead teacher will want to employ good techniques of storytelling.

Some basic techniques to keep in mind when telling a story are:

—Select stories suitable for the age child.

—Learn the events of the story in correct order.

—Avoid use of notes when telling the story.

—Tell the story with enthusiasm and expression.

—Prepare and learn a good opening sentence and a good concluding sentence.

—Maintain eye contact with the group while telling the story.

—Draw in the inattentive child by using his name in the story.

—Use conversation as much as possible.

—Let the story speak for itself—do not moralize at the end of the story.

—Create an informal setting when telling the story.

—Pause at the conclusion of the story to allow for children's comments before going to another activity.

9. *Learning games.*—Learning games become avenues through which much Bible content can be taught. Because boys and girls like to play games, they enjoy participating in Bible learning games. This approach can be used to help clarify content, the sequence of events, and even concepts relating to a unit of study. There are many variations to learning games. Usually the large group will be divided into two groups—each group composing a team. The teams may compete against each other. Another approach is for each group to designate a representative to play for them.

The television program "Concentration" provides a type framework around which a Bible learning game can be developed. For instance, if the purpose of the game is to learn ten Bible verses, prepare a "Bible Verse Concentration Game" with twenty squares. Place the first half of the Bible verse on one square and the last half on another. This is done until all squares are filled. Then mix them up, turn them over, and number 1–20. The pupil playing the learning game calls two numbers, the two squares are turned over to see if they match—completing a Bible verse (of course they must learn the Bible verses to identify them as correct matches). If the two do not match, the two squares are turned back over and another person or team gets a turn. This process is repeated until all of the Bible verses are correctly matched.

In preparing learning games, be sure to make the game large enough to be seen by the large group. Use the game with the workers

in a trial run prior to using it in the department. Carefully explain the rules for playing the game.

10. *Interviews.*—The interview provides a good setting for question-and-answer dialogue developed around unit outcomes. The interview can be with someone outside the group who may be classified as an "expert." The lead teacher may use an alternate approach of selecting a panel of pupils to do the interviewing.

For example, during a unit on missions, the lead teacher invites a missionary (who is home on furlough) to visit the department. Prior to the missionary's visit, both teachers and pupils compile a list of questions about areas of interest. These questions are collected, sorted out, and arranged as a basis for the interview. During the large group, the missionary is interviewed as he is asked such questions as:

(1) At what age did you decide to be a missionary?

(2) How long did it take you to learn Portugese?

(3) What is the thing you miss most by not living in America?

(4) What is the hardest thing for you to do as a missionary in another country?

(5) Tell us what boys and girls our age do in Brazil?

(6) Tell us about the church (mission station, hospital, etc.) where you work in Brazil?

Still another approach is to interview a person on tape away from the department. By using a tape recorder, the interview can be shared with the large group. One group utilized this approach by interviewing a number (4) of persons in the church on "What the Bible means to me." These interviews were taped at various times prior to the Sunday and then shared with the large group on Sunday morning.

The blend of role playing and interview can provide an interesting and stimulating experience. For example, Toby and Lawrence may pose as Paul and Timothy and answer questions directed to them in an interview.

11. *Orientation and/or report on field trip.*—A meaningful experience for a group to participate in is a field trip related to the area of study. A visit to a Jewish synagogue can aid the learner in knowing and understanding Jewish customs reflected in our Scriptures. If the entire group is making the field trip, the logical place to orient the group is during the large group in the department. On the other hand if only one of the small groups is making the field trip, allow them to report on the experiences to the large group following the trip.

12. *Music.*—As is true with worship, music is an intergal part of many large-group experiences. However, there are times when a unit lends itself to developing an entire large group session around music. Boys and girls are natural music lovers and participate enthusiastically. They enjoy singing familar hymns and respond positively to learning new songs. Discussing hymn texts causes music to have deeper meaning for boys and girls. Listening to a recording of songs (or hymns) provides an opportunity for the group to detect information requested prior to the listening session.

Theological concepts can be clarified through the use of songs/music. And yet music needs to be carefully selected to meet the needs of the age group. Some songs are so highly steeped in symbolism that they have little meaning to the literal-minded child. One first grader returning from a session at church began singing a song about her cup overflowing. When asked by her father what cup she was singing about, her reply was, "Oh, just a tea cup." Then her father asked what the cup was overflowing with and her reply was, "Oh, Daddy, coffee or tea—whatever you put in a cup."

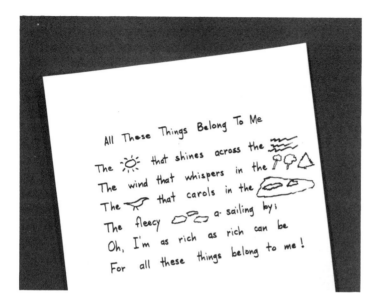

A good criterion for music to use with boys and girls is: the text is easily understood and the melody is singable and within the range of the children's voices.

Preparing a song rebus for use in the large group will aid in teaching the text. It will also help in visualizing the concepts. Select a song that has a good number of words that can be conveyed through pictures. Print the text of the song on a chalkboard or large sheet of paper, omitting the "picture" words. The pictures can then be distributed among the large group. As the children read the text, the individuals with the pictures come up and place them on the rebus in the right order. This process can be repeated if more drill is needed for the group to learn the text.

13. *Drama.*—Many forms of drama can be used to insure involvement in the large group. Acting out a Bible story helps the entire group to review the events in the story as well as reconstruct the events in the right order. This can be done impromptu or preplanned. For the lead teacher with limited experience in drama, backdrops and costumes should be omitted. It is important to remember the purpose—one of teaching and learning—not one of performing.

There are many types and variations of drama that can be wisely used in the large group. Some specific types of drama to consider using with the boys and girls in the large group to undergird the teaching purpose are role playing, pantomime, and puppets.

(1) Role playing may be done with little or no preparation on the part of the pupils. The teacher will describe a situation and identify pupils to play specific roles. At the desired place in the dialogue, the teacher will stop the role playing and the large group will then evaluate. This technique is particularly good when dealing in such areas as attitudes and behavior patterns.

For example, the lead teacher may ask three pupils to role-play the following situation:

Betty and Jo are sitting in their room at school before the class begins. They notice a new girl come into the room. She has on a faded dress that is definitely out of style. It is obvious that she is from a very poor family. Betty looks at Jo and says, "Who in the world is that? I hope she isn't assigned a seat next to me." As the teacher comes in, she cordially greets the new girl and then calls Betty and Jo over and says, "I want you to meet Sue Holland who is new in our school. While I run an errand, will you show her around and tell her about our school? (The three girls then carry on conversation from this point. At any point in the dialogue, the lead teacher will interrupt and then have the large group evaluate. What was good about the conversation? What should have been done [said] differently? If time permits, three other persons may be called on to role-play the same situation.)

(2) Pantomime is a technique that can be used to review Bible stories. For instance, if there are four small groups in the department, announce at the beginning of large group that each group will pantomime a different Bible story. The other groups watch and try to guess which Bible story it is. Of course the group pantomiming cannot speak a word during the presentation. In order to pantomime a story, each group must recall the Bible story and the personalities in the story.

(3) Puppets can be quickly made and used to convey both Bible stories, missions stories, and child-experienced situations. Some of the easier puppets to make are made from paper sacks, balloons, clothes hangers, and papier mâché. Again, this medium can be used as a method of recall or one of introduction of new stories.

The preceding suggestions for the large group not only give ideas for developing and structuring this segment of a teaching session. They also give examples through which relationships of the lead teacher to the other teachers can be established.

During the small-group period, each teacher is responsible for leading his group toward the same desirable outcomes through a project or activity. For instance, during a unit on missions in a third-grade department, the four small groups are each involved in a different project and these projects are being developed simultaneously in the same room:

Group one has been led in a study of several episodes in Paul's life. The group is now working on a rebus depicting some events in which missionary Paul was involved.

Group two is busy identifying Bible verses to put in a "missionary notebook." The group will then illustrate the Bible verses with drawings or pictures from the picture box. In planning the project, the third graders voted to give the "Missionary Notebook" to the children's ward in the local hospital.

Group three is engaged in making a "Who Am I Missionary Game." They have identified such Bible missionaries as Peter, Matthew, Luke, and Paul. To this list they added some other missionaries, such as Adonarium Judson, David Livingstone, and Lottie Moon. For each missionary, a description was written by the group, identifying clues. The last session of the unit, the small group will use the game in the large group.

Group four is planning to dramatize some events in the lives of of Timothy, Lydia, and Peter as three New Testament missionaries. The group first learned how these three were missionaries and then decided what part of each missionary's life they would dramatize. Excerpts from these three dramatizations will be shared with the large group as they are completed.

Important relationships among the teachers in the small groups begin to emerge. Each teacher recognizes his role in leading his small group toward the desirable outcomes for the unit. From unit planning, he is also aware of what other small groups are doing. Thus, he is not competing against the other teachers in the small groups, but joining efforts with them. He is assuming responsibility for his own small group, seeking to actively involve them in the planning of the project as well as carrying out of the plans.

As teaching plans are made, each teacher is also aware of large-group plans. Therefore duplication is avoided. At times he will ask the lead teacher for some time in the large group for his group to share with the entire department experiences they have had and knowledge they have gained.

In speaking to a group of Christian educators on "The Minister as Change Agent—20th Century Reformer," a teacher in theological education said the greatest thing a teacher brings to the teaching setting is himself—not his "bag of tricks." [7] Too often in teaching boys and girls, a teacher depends on his methods (his bag of tricks) rather than the sharing of himself and his encounter with God. Just what are the most desirable qualities in a teacher? The following list is only a beginning. Choose from it those that are more important and then add those qualities that you feel should be included:

Experiencing a vital relationship to God.—Teachers in Christian education should first of all have had an initial encounter with God through Jesus Christ that was life changing. Based on this life commitment to God, there should also be a daily encounter out of which a vibrant relationship to God exists. No methodology, gimmicks, or skills can be substituted for this continuing personal encounter with God. It is out of these ongoing experiences that rich teaching comes. Christian education is more than teaching facts; it is guiding the pupils to discover in God a way of life. Therefore, this daily discovery for the worker becomes essential in the pilgrimage of teaching children.

Growing as a person and as a teacher.—The person who stops growing and learning eventually stops teaching. Mere exposure to the boys and girls of today sparks learning. As conversation slips over into the area of space, science, and technology, the elementary age child often becomes the teacher and the adult the learner.

Working on a project during a unit on the creation story, Dan, Corky, and Stephen—all fifth graders—were preparing a mural on the solar system. Conversation centered on the idea that only God could create anything so wonderful and with such magnitude and precision. The boys were drawing the planets revolving around the sun when Dan turned and asked his teacher, "Should we draw the asteroids?" The confused teacher replied, "Dan, what are the aster-

[7] Elaine Dickson, "The Minister as Change Agent—20th Century Reformer." Lecture given at the Eastern Religious Education Association, Ridgecrest, North Carolina, July, 1970.

oids?" Dan answered, "We're not sure, but one theory is that a planet might have exploded and these are the particles rotating around the sun in a group."

The personal growth of the teacher will begin in a regular and systematic study of the Bible. Other areas of study and growth includes teaching/learning techniques, age-group characteristics and needs, and current events.

Developing a sensitivity toward the needs of others.—The teacher needs to develop the unique ability to sense the needs of others. This development begins with discovering the needs of those for whom he has responsibility in teaching, whether in the large group or the small group. However, it doesn't end with the pupils. This same sensitivity needs to be employed by teachers toward one another. Because teachers relate to one another in a team setting, isolation cannot be practiced. Fellow teachers, Mrs. Schwartz, senses Miss Brendle's insecurity as she accepts this new teaching position. Realizing Miss Brendle's need, Mrs. Schwartz loans her two books she has found helpful. She also arranges to view some filmstrips with her on teaching children. At the conclusion of the first unit, Mrs. Schwartz offers sincere words of commendation. This help is offered because the need was sensed and from it developd the bond of Christian friendship which should exist between all workers in a Christian education setting. The worker will also sense the needs among the pupils and then make teaching plans that will move toward meeting these needs.

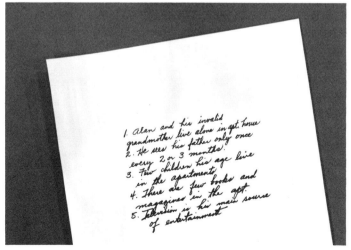

Second-grade Alan attends church irregularly. With uncombed hair and wrinkled clothes, he often seems withdrawn. The observant teacher discovered some of Alan's needs by observing him in the department and visiting in his home. The notes on the preceeding page were made by Alan's teacher. (What do these statements have to do with needs and how will they influence ways he can be taught?) What does all of this have to do with Christian education? Fortunately or unfortunately, we cannot "pull out" and minister to only Alan's spiritual needs. He must be dealt with as a total person. His lack of a desirable homelife affects his spiritual growth. The influence of a steady diet of violence on the television is directly affecting his development of a value system.

Assuming responsibility.—Each teacher in the Christian education setting needs to assume responsibility in the task of teaching. This will mean either being responsible for one of the small groups or the large group (if he is the lead teacher.) This also means being dependable. No teacher who assumes responsibility in the teaching task is absent without having made adequate provision for those in his group. This responsibility will also influence the way he makes preparation for teaching. In becoming a responsible person, he develops a high trust level toward the teachers with whom he teaches. He is open and honest in his evaluation of the department. He is able to take constructive criticism which is geared toward the overall improvement of the department.

Establishing and maintaining regular communication with the homes of boys and girls assigned to him.—A great deal of teaching can take place outside the classroom. This is especially true when contacts are made with the home. Regularly contacting the homes result in some important actions:

(1) The teacher gets to know Johnny better, which can aid in more effective teaching/learning setting.

(2) The family senses the importance and urgency of Christian education and will not only help Johnny attend regularly but hopefully will assume the responsibility of the home in training him.

(3) Johnny learns his teacher does really care about him and a bond of true friendship begins emerging.

Ideally, the initial contact with the home will be a visit, This visit may be followed up with postcards, notes, letters, birthday greetings, telephone calls, and so forth. A quarterly newsletter to parents provides an avenue for communication with the home. The following was used one quarter by a teacher of fifth and sixth graders:

December 13

Dear Mr. and Mrs. Moore:

We are having a good year in our department at church. I am glad Linda is a member of the group.

Our year began with six lessons on "Appreciating My Bible." During this unit the pupils drew a floor plan of the tabernacle, made a mural (a picture on a long piece of paper) ofthe tabernacle, and interviewed people asking them the question "Why do you appreciate the Bible?" We recorded their answers on tape and played the tape for the entire group.

Our next unit of study was "Thanking God for His Care." Each group chose one Bible character to study for four sessions. Linda's group chose Ruth. To learn more about her, we saw a film about Ruth, the pupils were given assignments (find out all you can about "Gleaning" in the fields, write a letter from Ruth to Orphah telling about life in Bethlehem), and we presented a play about Ruth using costumes and simple props.

The next unit will be "Honoring Jesus at Christmas" and we will spend four sessions studying the Christmas story. On December 15, we will have a breakfast and each person is asked to bring food, clothing, and fun gifts for one member of a very needy family.

Thank you for your part in helping Linda be faithful in attendance.

Sincerely,

Mrs. Ward

Mrs. Ward

Undergirding the total ministry of the church.—The teaching responsibility of workers with one group of children is only one part of the total ministry of the church. Each part of this total ministry should be seen in relationship to the other parts. Hopefully each teacher will view the sum of all parts. He will support this total ministry through participation and support. The child's knowledge of and interest in such areas as missions and music will often times be determined by the worker's enthusiasm for and knowledge about these.

The worker's teaching about worship, for instance, will be enhanced as he regularly participates in the worship services of the church. Boys and girls are quick to detect inconsistencies in our words and life patterns.

Possessing a genuine love and concern for boys and girls. Aside from life commitment to God, this is one of the most desirable qualities to look for in teachers with children. This is the underlying quality on which others mentioned above can be built. The person who possesses this genuine love for children will want to study and grow as a teacher; he will feel the urgency of developing and maintaining home contacts; he will discipline himself in an attempt to teach creatively. He will be sensitive toward others. In this context, this paraphrase of Phillips translation of 1 Corinthians 13 1:1–8 is appropriate:

"If I were to teach with the combined skill of men and angels, I should stir children like a fanfare of trumpets or the crashing of cymbals, but unless I had love, I should do nothing more. If I had the gift of forecasting the future and had in my mind not only all human knowledge but the secrets of God, and If, in addition, I had that absolute faith which can move mountains, but had no love, I tell you I should amount to nothing at all. If I were to sell all my possessions to feed hungry children and for my convictions, allowed my body to be burned, and yet had no love, I should achieve precisely nothing.

This love of which I speak is slow to lose patience—it looks for a way of being constructive. It is not possessive: it is neither anxious to impress nor does it cherish inflated ideas of its own importance.

Love has good manners and does not pursue selfish advantage. It is not touchy. It does not compile statistics of evil or gloat over the wickedness of other people. On the contrary, it is glad with all good men when Truth prevails.

Love knows no limit to its endurance, no end to its trust, no fading of its hope: It can outlast anything. It is, in fact, the one thing that still stands when all else has fallen.

CHAPTER FOUR
"BEGIN
WITH PLANNING"

A gaze off in the distance indicated Paula was probably deep in thought. Then with collected thoughts she began writing her report for the "Old-Old Times." The group had decided to assign each group member one of the Bible stories included in the unit. These Bible stories were being written in newspaper-article style and were to be included in their special edition of the "Old-Old Times."

Newspaper writing including Bible stories doesn't just happen! It must be planned—as is true with all approaches to good teaching. The planning process occurs at several levels; and when any level breaks down, the effectiveness of the teaching and learning is limited.

Levels of planning include overall or long-range objectives. These objectives (or goals) point us in the right direction. Our basic objectives in Christian education greatly influence our planning. These objectives become the foundation for all planning and give direction to what we plan.

To this level of long-range objectives, we add annual or seasonal plans. Many churches plan a calendar of activities for the year which may be the extent of long-range planning. Teaching plans will conform to this annual dated plan. Individual departments are not directly responsible for these larger areas of planning even though they should have opportunity for input. However, each department is directly influenced by this overall planning. Plans made by a department for boys and girls should be consistent with the church's overall planning and not contrary to or in conflict with it.

Department plans are added to the above levels. However at this point, there are two important aspects or segments—each heavily dependent upon the other. They are worker planning and pupil planning.

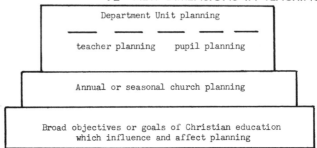

The above drawing presents the three basic levels of planning—two being done prior to the department planning. In churches where the first two levels are not done, individual departments can still plan for meaningful teaching and learning. The chapter will deal almost exclusively with this third level in the planning process—that of department planning.

Because of various tasks assigned to departments in addition to teaching, the administrative work will also need to be planned along with the teaching/learning experiences. However, because this book is dealing primarily with teaching, only the planning process of teaching will be dealt with.

Take the Long Look!

Before a team of teachers begins unit planning, there is merit overviewing the content for the year—or at least the quarter. Most curriculum plans are available for at least a year in advance. Most denominations and other publishers prepare curriculum resource books or pamphlets which may be secured well before a year begins. Sometimes these are purchase items for sale through denominational book stores. Others are free. Look at the subject areas being covered during the year. What blocks of Scripture will comprise the base on which the curriculum materials you will be using are built? How does this Bible content speak to specific needs of the individuals in the group? Is there *duplication* or omissions in the area of content? Do the concepts included in the curriculum plan fit the readiness of your pupils? Will pupils be challenged enough or will they be exploited?

Answering these valid questions will aid the team of teachers to thoughtfully talk through and evaluate the curriculum plan. It will avoid preempting units of study further down in the year. This type of annual planning will result in a thorough evaluation of your curriculum plan.

If you are not ready to move to an annual plan, consider at least a quarterly preview of your curriculum materials. Read the Scripture basis for the unit(s). Read and evaluate the learning projects or activities. Begin thinking about specific desired outcomes geared to your boys and girls. Try to see the unit(s) as a whole and not in segments or sessions. Some curriculum plans provide a guided study for individual teachers to preview the curriculum materials each quarter.[1]

Planning with the Teachers

The lead teacher has the responsibility of involving the other teachers in planning. As a bare minimum, the teaching team needs a planning meeting prior to the introduction of each new unit of study. (Hopefully the teaching team will be able to plan prior to each session and evaluate the previous session).

Just what is the purpose of the unit planning meeting? What should the teaching team accomplish through unit planning? Briefly, the following areas of work need to be accomplished by the team prior to introducing a new unit.

---

[1] Sunday School Foundation Series, Sunday School Board of the Southern Baptist Convention, Nashville, Tennessee.

1. *Evaluate the previous unit.*—A mandatory phase of planning is evaluation. Recognizing successes and failures helps teachers chart courses of action for the future. The following are questions you might answer in regard to a unit of study just completed:

(1) What desired outcomes did we express before beginning the unit?

(2) Did we conscientiously work toward our desired outcomes throughout the unit?

(3) Were these outcomes achieved?

(4) Which learning project(s) were most successful? Why?

(5) Which learning project(s) were least successful? Why?

(6) What were the strong points of the large group sessions?

(7) What were the weak areas of the large group sessions?

(8) Were schedules flexible enough to accomodate the teaching/learning process?

(9) How well did the teachers perform as a team? If the team did not "jell," where was the breakdown?

2. *Preview the unit to be introduced.*—Prior to the planning meeting each of the team should at least scan curriculum materials. The lead teacher may assign segments of the unit to different teachers, asking each one to preview his assignment at the planning meeting. For example the lead teacher could make the following assignments:

(1) Mr. Ashley—Review the Bible background for the four sessions.

(2) Mrs. Buckley—Review the learning projects suggested in the curriculum materials.

(3) Mr. Creech—Review the possible desired outcomes.

(4) Miss Price—Review resources suggested for the unit and identify those that are already available. Prepare a list of needed items.

(5) Mr. Brown—(lead teacher) Review large group plans.

Making such assignments thrusts each teacher into the study of at least part of the unit prior to the planning meeting. During the planning meeting, ask each teacher to share his report with the group. At the conclusion of the reports, the team has an overview of the unit to be introduced. This overview needs to be completed before specific assignments or responsibilities are discussed.

3. *Determine the desired outcome(s) for the unit.*—Most curriculum plans state a desired outcome(s) or aim(s) for the unit. Some of the more flexible curriculum plans offer a variety of outcomes

from which a teaching team may choose one or more. It is highly desirable for the teaching team to survey the suggested outcomes and then alter them where necessary. Or the team may write a completely new one designed to meet the specific needs of the boys and girls they teach. The needs, abilities, skills, and interests of the children should determine the approach and development of the unit of study. The desired outcome merely gives direction to both learners and teachers on ways the content will be handled.

In writing outcomes (aims) for a unit, Findley Edge gives three qualities of good aims or outcomes. They are:

(1) brief enough to be remembered

(2) clear enough to be written down

(3) specific enough to be achieved [2]

There are different kinds of desired outcomes or aims. Some of the more widely used desired outcomes for boys and girls may be placed in three groupings:

(1) Knowledge and understanding

These desired outcomes have to do with factual learning or understanding of factual information. Some samples of knowledge-and-understanding outcomes are:

—Learn some of the events in the life of Jesus.

—Know the names of twelve of Jesus' special helpers.

—List geographical locations where Jesus lived as a child.

2) Feelings and attitudes.

These desired outcomes are more difficult to measure than the knowledge outcomes. By carefully observing the boys and girls, one can detect changed attitudes and feelings. Some examples of feelings-and-attitude outcomes are:

—Feel that reading the Bible and talking to God pleases him.

—Respect the feelings and rights of others.

—Realize that some attitudes and feelings are acceptable, while others are not.

(3) Behavior and skills

These desired outcomes give direction in the area of improving skills or introducing new skills. They also speak in the area of behavior patterns. They may introduce new behavior patterns or reinforce desirable existing behavior patterns. Some samples are:

---

[2] Findley B. Edge, *Teaching for Results* (Nashville: Broadman Press, 1956), p. 92–93.

—Developing habits of working together cooperatively in the department.

—Grow in his ability to use the Bible by knowing the various divisions of the Bible and how to find them.

—Experience the joy of helping someone in need.

There are some units of study in which the knowledge-and-understanding aim will predominate. When your purpose is teaching factual information and where sequence is important, your aim or desired outcome will be knowledge and understanding. Other units of study deal heavily in attitudes and feelings. The study of some portions of the Bible causes one to be greatly moved. Still other units will result in improved skills and changed behavior patterns.

However, most units have some of each. There will usually be a blend of these three types of desired outcomes. Therefore, select the few that can be attained and plan the unit toward the fulfilment of these. Each learning project should undergird only one desired outcome. The large group experiences may speak to additional outcomes or merely reinforce those already identified by small groups. Be careful not to include too many desired outcomes. When this occurs, few, if any, will be attained. As a general rule, limit the number of desired outcomes from four to six per unit.

Each project, each large group experience, and each resource should support and undergird one or more of the outcomes selected. The outcomes become the criteria by which you evaluate what will be done during the unit and what will be eliminated. They also guide evaluation when the unit is completed.

4. *Select learning projects (activities)*.—There should be at least one learning project for each small group to participate in during the unit. Usually these learning projects (sometimes called Bible-learning projects or activities) last three or four sessions. However, if the small group finishes one, another project can be started.

Again, the selection of the learning projects will be determined by the unit outcomes. It is extremely important that the learning projects be looked upon and used as vehicles through which meaningful learning experiences emerge. The learning projects are not just something to do or something to keep the boys and girls busy until the "lesson begins." The learning projects become the very heart of the "lesson."

The teaching team needs to evaluate the learning projects suggested in the curriculum materials and determine those best suited to help the group reach the desired outcomes. Often this will require adapting learning projects to available resources as well as to group interest and skills. It could mean developing completely new ones. However, the better curriculum plans available to churches offer a variety of learning projects from which a teaching team can choose.

Hopefully, the department will be organized, limiting the maximum enrolment to thirty including workers. In a department of this size at least four small groups are needed. A learning project should be planned for every four to six pupils. In the better curriculum plans, eight or more learning projects are suggested which means there will be twice as many suggestions as the department can use. This variety makes it possible for workers who feel less creative to still have a large selection from which they can choose the four or five projects needed.

For example, on the unit "Three Busy Years" where fifth and sixth graders are to be involved in a study of the three years of Jesus' public ministry, the following Bible-learning projects might appear in a good curriculum plan:

(1) *Map drawing.*—This group will prepare a large map showing the journeys of Jesus during one of the three years of his public ministry. If time permits, the group may choose to draw a map for each of the three years. Large sheets of newsprint or wrapping paper may be used, or the group may decide to use a cloth sheet and wax crayons. If the first year of Jesus' ministry is chosen, the following references may be used:

a. From Nazareth to Bethabara: Matthew 3:13
b. From Bethabara to the Wilderness of Judea: Matthew 4:1
c. From the Wilderness to Bethabara: John 1:38–51.
d. From Bethabara to Cana: John 1:43
e. From Cana to Capernaum: John 2:12
f. From Capernaum to Jerusalem: John 2:13 for the Passover
g. From Jerusalem to the tour of Judea: John 3:22
h. From the Judean tour to Jacob's well at Sychar: John 4:3–5
i. From Samaria to Cana in Galilee: John 4:43–46
j. From Cana to Nazareth: Luke 4:16–27

The group will decide how the map is to be drawn and by whom.

(2) *Newspaper writing.*—The group will write a newspaper that might have been published in Jesus' day. The newspaper will feature headlines and articles about the different miracles performed by Jesus. Pupils could draw pictures and illustrations. The dateline for each article will be the place where the miracle or event was performed. The following references may be used to supply the necessary information for the articles: Matthew 8:5–13; Matthew 9:27–31; John 5:1–16; Luke 17:11–19; Matthew 12:9–13; Luke 22:17–22; Matthew 8:14–17; Mark 2:1–12.

(3) *Drama.*—Let this group dramatize one or more of the miracles performed by Jesus as described in these verses: Mark 4:35–41; Mark 6:30–44; Matthew 14:24–33; Luke 5:1–11; John 11:1–44. If the group wishes to use costumes, curtain material, old pieces of cloth, towels, and so forth can be used. However, drama can be very effective without costumes.

The group will need to do careful research and be familiar with the characters. Then they need to act as they feel the character would have acted, speak as the characters would have spoken, and "stay in character." Let the group evaluate their drama on this basis. Each drama can be done two or three times, using different pupils.

At the completion of group work on the drama, the group may wish to dramatize at least one miracle for the large group so all may benefit from the study.

(4) *Crucifixion-resurrection study.*—The group working on this project will study the events that happened to Jesus during the week prior to his crucifixion and resurrection. This group can effectively use a harmony of the Gospels, a Bible dictionary, and a Bible concordance. The group may choose to prepare a chart giving the events in chronological order. If so, the chart could look like this:

Chronology of Jesus' Last Week of Public Ministry

Sunday (Palm)	
Monday	
Tuesday	
Wednesday	
Thursday	
Friday	
Saturday	
Sunday	

(5) *Burial customs.*—This group will study the burial customs of the Jewish people during Bible times. You will need to have available research tools for this group, such as Bible dictionaries and books on life in Bible times. Perhaps the group could do some of its work in the church library. The group will list or draw pictures of customs to share with the department. Their study should answer the following questions: (1) Who prepared the body for burial? (2) Where were the people buried? (3) How were the rich buried differently from the poor? (4) What type of funerals did the people have? (5) What was the general attitude toward death?

As these questions are answered, let the group read from a recent translation (such as TEV) the story of Jesus' burial in Joseph of Arimathaea's tomb and also the account of Jesus and Lazarus.

(6) *Hymn search.*—This group will search for hymns about the life of Jesus. These hymns can be read (or sung) carefully with special thought given to the hymn texts. Then list the hymns in categories. One or more of the following categories may be chosen: Jesus' birth, Jesus' ministry, Jesus' death, Jesus' resurrection. Let the group select one or two hymns to be sung each Sunday in the large group. The small group may choose to learn a new hymn and teach it to the department.

(7) *Choosing the twelve.*—This group will make a study of the twelve apostles Jesus chose as his special helpers. The group will name the twelve apostles (Matt. 10:2; Mark 3:16; Luke 6:14; Acts 1:13) and will learn about their call to special work (Mark 1:17, 20; Mark 2:14; Luke 6:13; John 1:43; Acts 22:21). After getting the scriptural base for this study, the group will do research to find as much information as possible about each apostle.

The group may then develop a "Who Am I?" game. Each person in the group will write a brief description about one or more of the apostles. This learning game may first be played in the small group and later shared in the large group. An example of the game is:

I am a native of Galilee. I am well educated and was wealthy. But I did not have many friends until after I became a disciple. There is a book in the Bible that has my name. Before becoming a follower of Jesus, I was a publican or tax collector and money changer. My name used to be Levi. *Who am I?* (Matthew)

If time permits, the group may choose to display the information learned about the twelve apostles on a chart, make a frieze or act out a scene from the life of an apostle.

(8) *Appearances of Jesus after resurrection.*—This group will do research to determine the appearances Jesus made from the day of his resurrection to his ascension. There could be as many as eleven (11) assignments or these may be combined for fewer assignments. Such assignments as the following could be given:

a. Seen by Mary Magdalene—Luke 20:11–18
b. Seen by other women—Matthew 28:9
c. Seen by Peter—1 Corinthians 15:5
d. Seen by two disciples—Luke 24:15–31
e. Seen by ten apostles (Thomas absent)—John 20:19,24
f. Seen by seven disciples fishing—John 21:1–24
g. Seen by eleven apostles—Matthew 28:16–17
h. Seen by five hundred brethern—1 Corinthians 15:6
i. Seen by James—1 Corinthians 15:7
j. Seen by eleven apostles—Acts 1:2–9

This group may decide for each person with an assignment to write a short story in first person about his encounter of seeing Jesus.

Or, group may decide to prepare a chart like the following to share with the large group:

TIME	SEEN BY	PLACE

In the unit planning meeting, the workers will study all of the learning projects. Then with the desired outcomes, the interests, and previous department experiences of the pupils in mind, learning projects for the unit will be discussed. The workers may decide which Bible-learning projects to use or the decision may be made by the pupils on the first session of a unit—when the unit is introduced and unit planning with the pupils is done.

However, the detailed planning of each learning project cannot be done until the first session of a unit when the pupils who are working on the project can be involved.

5. *Plan the large-group experiences.*—No unit planning is complete until the total teaching period has been carefully planned. Approximately one half or more of each teaching session will be spent in the small groups where the learning projects are being developed. The remaining time will be spent in the large group—usually with the lead teacher responsible. The learning experiences which begin in the small groups must be carried on in the large group. Here the teachers reinforce each other's efforts. Segments are tied together meaningfully. Ideas are clarified. Misconceptions are corrected.

Involvement of the learner is essential. Therefore, the lead teacher must know about each of the learning projects in the small groups. Coordinated plans must be made with the team of teachers.

The large-group session must not be allowed to become a lecture, sermonette, or a "talking down to" period. It must not be a closing exercise or closing assembly. But it must be an exciting learning encounter, involving the total group. To do this, the lead teacher will plan—

- Music and worship experiences consistent with the desired outcomes for the unit.
- Sharing from the small groups as learning projects are completed.
- Preview of material relevant to the unit.
- Presentation of Bible background significant to the areas of study.
- Related Bible and child-experience stories and situations.
- Review of materials covered in the unit.

The methods used in the large group should demand involvement of each person. Learning games, music, filmstrips, role playing, drama question/answer (both verbal and written) will draw the pupils into the learning situation in the large group. Plan informal structure of the large group. A relaxed atmosphere doesn't just happen—it must be planned!

The seating in the large group should be informal, perhaps in a semicircle or around tables. If he can be seen by the entire group, the lead teacher may even remain seated as he conducts the large group. A conversational tone (rather than lecture) should be employed by the lead teacher. This informal setting will invite responses from the group. Dialogue will emerge spontaneously.

Write Your Plans

The unit planning meeting involving only the teachers isn't complete until plans are written. Each teacher will want to keep his own notes and write his own plans. However, the use of a simple unit plan sheet will be helpful for the team. The plan sheet is given only as an example. Adapt it to meet your needs. (Remember plan sheets are to serve the teacher and not the teacher to serve the plan sheet).

Planning with the Pupils

Up to this point, only the foundational planning has been achieved. The most vital aspect of planning is the level in which the boys and girls are involved. Because of this necessity, the schedule for the

```
                    Unit Plan Guide
            (to be filled in by each teacher on the team)
    Unit Title _____

    Desired Outcome _____

    _____

    Projects or Activities to Fulfil Desired Outcomes:
    Small Group 1                    Project
     (teacher)          _____

    Small Group 2
     (teacher)          _____

    Small Group 3
     (teacher)          _____

    Small Group 4
     (teacher)          _____

    Large Group Plans   _____, lead teacher
    Session 1
    _____

    _____

    _____
```

```
Session 2
_____
_____
_____


Session 3
_____
_____
_____


Session 4
_____
_____
_____


Materials Needed                    Teacher Responsible
_____        _____
_____        _____
_____        _____
_____        _____
```

first session of a unit varies from the schedule for the remaining sessions. Schedules must always remain flexible. The following is one approach that can be used the first session of a unit. (This schedule is based on an hour to an hour and thirty minutes for a session.)

10–20 minutes—*Small Groups* (Each smaller group participates in learning games and puzzles related to the subject area [content] of the unit to be introduced.)

30–45 minutes—*Large Group* (The Bible material for this session is presented, along with an overview of unit, sharing of the desired outcomes with the group, and identification of the learning projects to be done by small groups.)

20–25 minutes—*Small Group Planning* (Each small group will make detail plans on how its learning project will be developed; how each member of the small group will be involved, etc.)

Now, let's go back and look at each segment of this first session of a new unit. Notice how individuals are involved in making decisions. Remember intelligent decisions cannot be made unless the group as a whole knows the desired outcome for the unit. Each phase of the work on this first session should be held together by the desired outcome. In other words, the desired outcome becomes the criteron by which we evaluate what will and will not be done during the sessions of the unit.

Small-group learning (10–15 minutes).—In departments where permanent groupings are used, the boys and girls will go directly to their assigned teacher. However in departments where temporary groupings are used, pupils will choose the introductory activities in which they want to work and will join that particular group. In most departments, the entire group does not arrive at the same instant. Joe and Beth come early. Susan may arrive five minutes later. Jeff is nearly always late. Therefore, why wait until Jeff arrives to begin?

If we begin with the large group, we need to wait until most of the boys and girls arrive. But teaching can begin with only one pupil. For this period of small group work, plan activities that can either be completed or cut off in ten to fifteen minutes. The content or subject matter for these activities will be developed around the area or theme of the new unit being introduced. Puzzles and learning games that can be played individually or in a small group are especially good to use during this first small-group time. This teaching can be done with only one or two and it can also be done with the entire small group (6 or 7).

Another type learning game may be made of flash cards with a key word or phrase on one side of the card. The word phrase, based on the forthcoming or present unit of study should call forth additional information from the pupil. The game may be played by two teams or just two individuals. It can be a technique used in pretesting and also later in review.

If Bible games are homemade, prepare them so they can be used again by another pupil. For instance, the following crossword puzzle could be used when introducing a unit on the life of Jesus. To make the game reusable, cover it with acetate (plastic) and have each player use a grease pencil (china marker). When a player completes the game, the answers may be wiped off with a tissue and the game is ready for another person to use.

LEARNING ABOUT JESUS

Across
2. Town where Jesus was born.
7. Place where Baby Jesus slept.
8–9. Men from the East who traveled to Bethlehem to see Jesus when he was several months old.
11. Men who kept sheep and to whom the angels told of Jesus' birth.

Down
1. Guided the Wise Men to Bethlehem.
3. A book in the New Testament that tells the Christmas story.
4. Word meaning a large number, Luke 2:13.
5. Mother of Jesus.
6. Heavenly bodies who appeared to the shepherds.
10. Where there was no room for Mary and Joseph.
12. Ruling king of Palestine when Jesus was born.

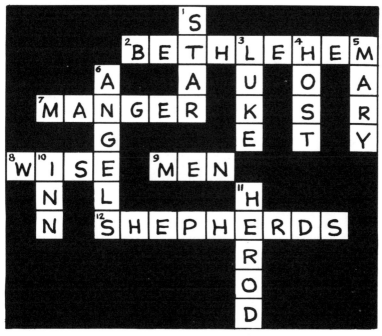

Other types of learning games that can be effectively used to introduce a unit of study are:

Matching words with pictures
Matching answers with questions
Shaped puzzles (especially good with first and second graders)
Jumbled words
Bible hopscotch
Bible baseball or football
Spelling bee idea with question and answers
Picture hunt
Identifying Bible verses with pictures
Whispering game

By the time each small group has been involved for ten to fifteen minutes in several types of learning experiences, interest will have been aroused concerning the subject area of the unit. Questions will be asked. A desire to learn more will be evident. This type of readiness can be achieved in the first small group.

Large-group planning (30–45 minutes).—During this large group, the lead teacher will usually be responsible. There will be elements of worship built in (music, prayer, and so on). The lead teacher will then guide an overview of the unit. The setting or background for the unit should be given. This could include customs of the times being studied, the geographical setting, the political scene, or fitting the unit chronologically into history. The entire unit should be seen as a whole by the group. (One person has defined a unit as one lesson that extends for several sessions.) The group should then be made aware of the learning goals (desired outcomes). For the first and second grader, these will be translated into language meaningful to this age child. Care should be taken to express the learning goals in a way that is meaningful to the pupil, whether first or sixth grader. The lead teacher may state these by saying for example, "Here are some things we want to learn about Jesus this month. . . . ," or, "At the end of the next four weeks let's see if we know . . ." These learning goals should be stated (simply and briefly) on a poster where all can see and the poster left up in the room during the entire unit. In many units there will be a number of different learning goals from which the group may choose. This choice should not always be limited to the teachers. Boys and girls can help identify learning goals as long as those being offered are of equal value.

Another important segment of the large group is identifying the learning projects in which the small groups will participate. There are several methods by which this can be achieved:

(1) The learning projects can be suggested by the boys and girls.

(2) The learning projects can be listed by the teachers for the boys and girls.

After the learning projects are identified, boys and girls need to be grouped for participation and learning. There are two basic ways of achieving this grouping:

(1) Each pupil can choose the learning project on which he will work during the entire unit.

(2) Each pupil can be assigned to one of the learning projects on which he will work during the entire unit.

Regardless of the approach used, the learning projects should be identified in the large group more by content area or experience rather than by the methodology to be used. For instance, "Mr. Jones and his group will be learning about how Jesus helped sick people as they prepare the frieze" rather than "Mr. Jones' group will make a frieze." Then during small-group planning, the pupils can decide on the media and methods to be used in developing the learning project. This is particularly true with the older elementary age child who can delve into more cognitive learning. Because his analyzing and evaluation thinking is being developed there will be more possibilities open to the older child.

After each learning project has been identified and each pupil knows which one he will be working on, the large group will dissolve into small groups for the detailed planning.

Small-group planning (20–25 minutes).—By this time, each member of the group will have had the benefit of the learning activities at the beginning of the session and of the overview of the unit. He will be aware of the learning goals for the unit and will also know the various learning projects being done in the department.

Now each small group needs to talk about the project on which it will work. It is very important that the boys and girls be involved in the decision-making at this level. They should answer such questions as:

—How will the project be developed (made)?

—What will each member of the group do?

—What information (research) does the group need?

—What materials are needed by the next session?

Again plans need to be written. The following planning guide may be used by each teacher meeting with a small group. The first two questions are to be answered by the teacher while the other questions are to be answered by the entire small group.

Small Group Plan Guide

(to be filled in by each teacher who leads a small group)

Project _____ Teacher _____

What do I want the group to learn from this project? _____

_____

What information do I need to introduce this project? _____

_____

(to be filled in by both teacher and pupils during small group planning)

What do we want to learn through this project? _____

_____

How are we going to develop (make) this project? _____

_____

What will each person do on this project?

Name   Responsibility

_____   _____

_____   _____

_____   _____

What materials do we need for the next session? _____

_____

What research (assignments) needs to be done and by whom? __

_____

The importance of the planning process cannot be overemphasized. Meaningful learning must be carefully planned. The learner and the teacher must become a team in the planning process. Both must be aware of where they are going and how they are going to get there. Participation/involvement of the group is a prerequisite to desirable learning.

All phases of the planning process may not be achieved at first. Work toward developing your unique approach to planning that will result in desirable learning. Teachers in a department cannot become a team until they learn to plan together. This team approach cannot fully realize effective teaching until teachers learn to involve the pupils in the planning process.

Begin now with good planning!

CHAPTER FIVE
"LEARNING
IS EXCITING"

All six of the eleven-year-olds had successfully given the Ten Commandments from memory. Mr. Leber, the teacher, was a strong believer in memory work. He was not content until every pupil in his group showed evidence of successfully memorizing the suggested Scripture passages.

Two days later these same boys sat in school, absorbed in their work, when the 3:00 o'clock dismissal bell rang. Shortly afterwards Jerry and Mike strolled into the corner grocery on their way home. Jerry gave the clerk his money for a candy bar and left. Mike pretended to look at the comic books until the clerk went into the stockroom. Quickly, and without leaving any money, Mike took a candy bar and hurried out of the store. On the way home, he ate his stolen merchandise.

At church both boys had successfully said the Ten Commandments. Both boys had said, "Thou shalt not steal." However, one boy had not learned with understanding. Mike's learning had not changed the way he thought and acted. Merely repeating words from memory doesn't guarantee that learning with understanding has taken place. Learning with understanding goes far beyond memorizing or rote learning.

A great deal has been said and written about learning. Some educators have classified levels of learning ranging from the least desirable to the most desirable. Unfortunately, much of Christian education has been at the level of rote or memory with out regard to understanding. It has been only a catechism which has not affected behavior patterns or attitudes. Effective Christian education must go beyond memory for the sake of learning facts. It must be learning with understanding.

. . . Katona[1] demonstrated the superiority of learning by

---

[1] Program director of the survey and research center and professor of economics and pyschology, University of Michigan.

understanding over learning by memorizing. Let us recall his findings. What has been understood will be held in memory far longer than like material that has been memorized. Furthermore, we are able to apply what we have understood much more widely than what we have memorized—so much so that, as we have seen, transfer (or the application of learned material to new cases) may be used as a test of understanding. This is no small advantage at a time when knowledge is accumulating so rapidly that no one has enough time in school to learn what a well-informed person needs to know. Again, learning by understanding is often more economical than memorizing; even apart from transfer, we can frequently acquire more material in a given time in this way. Besides, a child will soon lose interest in memorizing, while understanding holds his interest and attention much longer.[2]

There are a few cases when memorization is in order. For instance, in helping boys and girls develop the skill of using their Bibles, memorizing the books of the Bible (in correct order) becomes meaningful. Thus memorization is equipping them for a skill development. The use of this skill will open many opportunities for learning with understanding.

How can learning with understanding take place? Does this completely rule out memory work? How can learning at church take place in such a way that the learner will later transfer his learnings into everyday life situations?

There is no easy formula that always guarantees learning with understanding. Learning must become an exciting adventure both for the teacher and the learner if learning with understanding takes place. This learning must actively involve both the learner and the teacher. Where possible, content must be experienced firsthand. Where it cannot be experienced, content should be role-played or dramatized, even though this is once removed from the actual experience. Films, filmstrips, closed circuit TV are also good substitutes for the actual experiences. Telling or hearing about the experience alone is the least desirable.

Learning can be exciting in the field of Christian education. At times memorization is necessary and desirable but it must always

---

[2] Alexander Frazier, editor, *The New Elementary School* (Association for Supervision and Curriculum Development, NEA, Washington, 1968), p. 19.

be coupled with understanding. For learning to be exciting, there must be on the part of the learner active involvement, understanding, and application.

Perhaps in the following illustrations of Bible-learning projects you will sense how involvement, understanding, and application were achieved.

The Psalms are now much more meaningful to Sandy, a third grader. She not only knows the Psalms are in the Bible and how to find this portion in her Bible, but she has been led in such exciting learning that she wrote a psalm herself:

A Psalm

I know God loves and cares for me
because God gave us beautiful sights to see
and touch, smell and taste.
I know God loves and cares for me
because he made the stars
as guides for us to find our way.
I know God loves and cares for me
because he encouraged men to love each other.
I know God loves and cares for me
because he made beautiful things
for our eyes to see
while he was on earth
and he made animals to see,
feel, and to play with,
a sunset to watch at night,
in autumn beautiful colored leaves
to watch fall, winter snow to play in,
spring the starting of flowers, and
growing of new plants,
summer a time to play.
While these four seasons go by
and start again, we should try to
go to church—
also known as "God's house." [3]

Learning with understanding begins as pupils are involved even in the planning process. Thinking is challenged, ideas expressed,

---

[3] Baptist Leader, September, 1970. © Copyright 1970 the American Baptist Board of Education and Publication. Used by permission.

and a plan of action decided upon. This plan must be from the group and not just the teacher. As learning projects are agreed upon, assignments of work are made to involve the total group.

For instance, when a unit was introduced on Peter's encounter with Jesus, the pupils learned that much of the setting would be in a town named Capernaum. The group then decided to draw a mural of Capernaum. As they discussed how the mural would be developed, questions were formed by both children and teacher. The following questions had to be answered before the work on the mural could begin:

1. Where is Capernaum located?
2. What kind of background needs to be drawn (flat land, hillsides, seashore?)
3. Is it a city, town, or village?
4. What types of trees and other vegetation should be in the picture?
5. What kind of houses were in Capernaum at this time?

Suddenly the drawing of this mural provoked serious study of a New Testament town. Producing the mural became more than just the busy work of drawing a picture. The mural provided an avenue through which learning with understanding could take place. Assignments were made; research was completed; and with colored chalk and newsprint the group drew their findings. Later as the group studied about Jesus visiting in the home of Peter to heal his mother-in-law, each child had a specific mental image of the setting for this Bible story—because some exciting learning had taken place.

During a unit on the teachings of Jesus, one small group was involved in studying the parable of the prodigal son (Luke 15:11–32). Immediately the teacher was faced with the question of how to bring about learning with understanding, not just mere learning of facts.

Remembering the necessity of group involvement, Mr. Peters, the teacher, invited the group to read the Scripture from Luke 15 from three different translations. After a comparison of the three, Jerry volunteered to bring a report at the next session on the word "parable." With a clearer understanding that Jesus often told stories (parables) to illustrate truths he wished people to understand, the group talked about ways they could analyze this parable.

Jeff, the quiet one in the group, suggested that they divide the story into parts. Mark, who likes to draw, said the group could draw each part of the story.

In response to these comments, Mr. Peters said, "If we draw a series of pictures on one piece of paper and put them in the right order, we'll have a frieze." This struck a responsive note from the small group and they agreed to record their findings in the form of pictures on a frieze.

The five group members decided to divide the parable into the following parts to illustrate on the frieze:

Part One: The father and his two sons are living together on the father's farm.

Part Two: The younger son, having just received his inheritance, is starting to leave home.

Part Three: The younger son, now away from home, is running out of money and begins looking for work and food.

Part Four: The younger son finds work—that of feeding pigs. He gets his food from the food given to the pigs.

Part Five: The younger son realizes he would be better off as a servant for his father. He knows that he has sinned and done wrong. With this knowledge and feeling, he decides to return home, ask for forgiveness, and work as a servant for his father.

The thinking and planning of this frieze are an important part of the learning process. They provide a framework around which much conversational teaching takes place. Individuals try out new ideas, subject to the evaluation of the group and teacher. Completing a frieze usually takes several sessions. Not only is it important to complete the frieze and learn the story of the prodigal son, it is more important to learn what this story means. (Because this story involves more abstract concepts it would probably be used only with older elementary-age children).

Upon completing their project, the group shared the frieze with the large group. Each group member told about his section of the frieze.

During a unit on nature, a group of second and third graders were involved, not only in studying about God's creative power but in expressing their thinking about God's world. One small group decided it would prepare some original poems (creative writing) about God's world. In addition to the poems, each person would also bring something to display on a nature table during the unit.

Through this experience, the teacher involved the group in learning with understanding. It is one thing for a second grader to quote Genesis 1:1, "In the beginning God created the heaven and the earth." However when this same second grader can transfer this knowledge to the now as he sees a beautiful rose and recall that only God can make the rose, learning with understanding has been achieved.

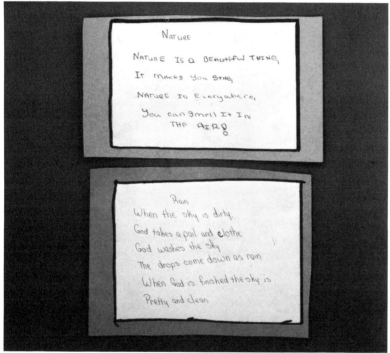

This type of learning takes time. It cannot be hurried or rushed. The creative writing shown above was done over a period of three or four sessions. It becomes the vehicle through which effective conversational teaching occurs.

Usually boys and girls in grades four through six can handle memory work without too much difficulty. However, a word of caution needs to be expressed. Memory work without understanding is far from desirable. Merely being able to repeat words in a certain order does not change behavior or attitudes. Therefore, when memory work is desired, be sure to take the time to interpret the meaning of the verse, passage, or other material. Then give the pupils time to question. If possible, have the pupils reconstruct the thoughts or ideas in their own words.

During a Christmas unit, a group had spent some time learning verses from Luke 2. After each pupil had successfully repeated the verses, Cheryl asked, "What does 'house and lineage of David' mean?" How unfortunate it would have been had all the time been spent on learning to repeat the words and then the children not know what the words were really saying.

The interpretation or explanation of verses to be memorized should precede the rote learning. Using this same Scripture passage from Luke 2, another teacher prepared a large piece of paper with references of four of the key verses written on it. As the pupils arrived for this session, each was asked to look up in the Bible one of the references and then draw a picture illustrating the verse. Through these four pictures, the group was led in a discussion of the Christmas story. Words and phrases were clarified. Questions were answered. Mental pictures portrayed the events in the story. With this background, the group then committed to memory the beautiful words Luke used in telling the Christmas story. There was learning with understanding.

Another group of boys and girls was being introduced to a new unit of study about Paul's life. Immediately, there were questions about words the boys and girls did not understand. When this occurs, can there be learning with understanding? So in addition to the planned Bible-learning project, the small group decided to prepare an illustrated dictionary, listing the words unfamiliar to them. This dictionary would later be shared with the large group in the department.

During the four sessions of the unit whenever an unfamiliar word was discovered, it was added to the dictionary. One person would take the word, look it up in a dictionary, and then draw a picture to illustrate and help define it.

One of the most dramatic stories of the Old Testament involves the life of Moses. The Pharaoh commanding all male babies to be put to death; the king's daughter dramatically rescuing this Hebrew infant and later providing Moses with the best education available at that time; the constant struggle Moses faced between his Hebrew background and his Egyptian training; his escape from Pharaoh and life as a shepherd; his return to Egypt and encounter with Pharaoh to let the Hebrews leave and the final exodus and wanderings in the wilderness.

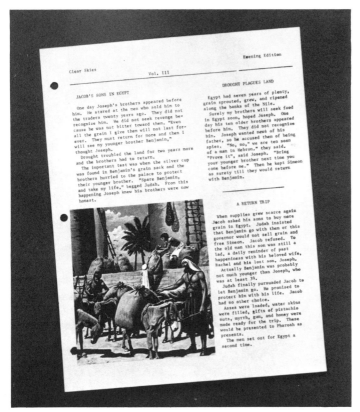

There are so many facets to the story of Moses' life it is difficult to capture all of these aspects in one unit of study. However, one group of elementary-age boys and girls learned with understanding through the following Bible-learning project. The medium used was the development of a newspaper, named by the group "The Egyptian Times." So involved were they in this project, the boys and girls decided not to stop with a handwritten edition but to type the articles and put them in a bound notebook. Each person in the small group was commissioned as a reporter and the news stories began coming in! Research, map study, biblical customs, Hebrew life styles all had to be studied. These actions led to more than merely learning facts; feelings and emotions were aroused. A sense of God's direction in Moses' life was felt. The page above is an example of the results from this learning experience. The important thing in this learning project is not the finished product (newspaper); it is the learning experiences that occurred as the newspaper was being developed—the thinking, the analyzing, the reconstructing of the story, the feeling and emotions aroused; the sensing of God working and moving through people to bring about his change in history. The newspaper (or any medium) becomes only the framework through which learning with understanding takes place. Once the project is completed, dispose of the medium (newspaper, in this instance), for it will have served its purpose.

Have you ever looked at yourself through the eyes of your pupils? Do you know what the learner wants in a good teacher. Teacher-learner relationships determine the degree to which learning with understanding is achieved. In a survey made by an editor of children's materials, boys and girls were asked to write the editor and identify what they wanted in a good teacher at church.[4] Each response came from a different pupil in grades four through seven from over the nation. Don't worry about the scale for now. Just read the following responses taken from this survey:

	Low				High
—Can pronounce words good.	1	2	3	4	5
—Exciting.	1	2	3	4	5
—If "proved" wrong will give in and say no.	1	2	3	4	5
—Sweet but strict.	1	2	3	4	5
—Teaches the best he knows how.	1	2	3	4	5
—One who is very extraordinary.	1	2	3	4	5
—One that sometimes will have fun with you.	1	2	3	4	5
—One that knows what you're capable of.	1	2	3	4	5
—One that can do more than you think he can.	1	2	3	4	5
—One that you learn from continually.	1	2	3	4	5
—Willing to listen.	1	2	3	4	5
—Arouses ideas in others.	1	2	3	4	5
—Generous of time.	1	2	3	4	5
—You can always laugh with a good teacher.	1	2	3	4	5
—A teacher that can teach well about God, and teach you to learn so that you can keep it in mind and not forget it.	1	2	3	4	5
—A good teacher has to believe in the Lord Jesus Christ and love everyone.	1	2	3	4	5

[4] Survey conducted by W. Mark Moore, editor of children's materials, Sunday School department, Sunday School Board of the Southern Baptist Convention, 1969.

	Low				High
—When he is sick he has a substitute.	1	2	3	4	5
—One who is not fussy!	1	2	3	4	5
—Be able to talk so that kids can understand.	1	2	3	4	5
—Be funny sometimes.	1	2	3	4	5
—Carries over lessons from Sunday to Sunday.	1	2	3	4	5
—A teacher that makes learning fun.	1	2	3	4	5
—One who knows pupil's abilities.	1	2	3	4	5
—Not grouchy, but happy.	1	2	3	4	5
—Doesn't get steamed over some little thing.	1	2	3	4	5
—He should be able to accept responsibility.	1	2	3	4	5
—Should be able to keep control of the pupils and himself.	1	2	3	4	5
—One who does not break promises.	1	2	3	4	5
—One who is firm to the mean people, and nice to the other people, and has no pets to make the other people jealous.	1	2	3	4	5
—One who has understanding of this younger generation.	1	2	3	4	5
—One who will give us responsibility.	1	2	3	4	5
—One who is neat in appearance.	1	2	3	4	5
—Means what they say.	1	2	3	4	5
—Is always on time.	1	2	3	4	5
—One who has wisdom through experience.	1	2	3	4	5
—Sets a good example.	1	2	3	4	5
—Gives attention to pupils needs.	1	2	3	4	5
—Directs learning.	1	2	3	4	5
—Have good posture.	1	2	3	4	5
—Be willing to learn with the class.	1	2	3	4	5
—Teachers who have confidence in the pupils.	1	2	3	4	5
—One who encourages us to visit others.	1	2	3	4	5
—One who uses the Bible every Sunday.	1	2	3	4	5
—They don't do things themselves that pupils can do.	1	2	3	4	5
—Be willing to help slower students.	1	2	3	4	5
—One who teaches manners.	1	2	3	4	5
—A teacher that prays.	1	2	3	4	5
—Reasons out problems with pupils.	1	2	3	4	5
—A teacher who tries to increase his own knowledge.	1	2	3	4	5
—One who listens to pupils ideas.	1	2	3	4	5
—Gives work on pupils' level.	1	2	3	4	5

	Low				High
—A teacher who plans.	1	2	3	4	5
—If he has a headache, he shouldn't take it out on his pupils.	1	2	3	4	5
—The teacher shouldn't talk too much, but let the pupils say something.	1	2	3	4	5
—One who accepts criticism.	1	2	3	4	5
—One who teaches instead of wasting time.	1	2	3	4	5
—One who is not bossy.	1	2	3	4	5
—A teacher who will experiment with new things.	1	2	3	4	5
—Teachers who do not hurry us.	1	2	3	4	5
—One who is understanding, and who we can tell our problems to and who can help us overcome our weaknesses.	1	2	3	4	5
—A teacher who praises pupils in their loyalty in coming to church.	1	2	3	4	5
—A teacher who speaks our own language.	1	2	3	4	5
—One who has patience; is sensible and sees that we do our assignments.	1	2	3	4	5
—One who is in a good mood at least at the start of the day!	1	2	3	4	5
—One who is nice smelling, clean inside and outside.	1	2	3	4	5
—A teacher who smiles.	1	2	3	4	5
—One who doesn't always stick to the book.	1	2	3	4	5
—A teacher who doesn't humiliate you.	1	2	3	4	5
—A teacher who is prepared and likes what he is doing.	1	2	3	4	5
—Active in church activities.	1	2	3	4	5
—A teacher that helps you learn things you never knew before.	1	2	3	4	5
—They should have fun teaching.	1	2	3	4	5
—One who is a thinker.	1	2	3	4	5
—One who keeps the room attractive.	1	2	3	4	5
—One who worries about you.	1	2	3	4	5
—Does things with the lesson besides read it.	1	2	3	4	5
—A *good teacher* has *good pupils!*	1	2	3	4	5

Learning with understanding certainly involves both the teacher and the learner. Too often we think of teacher qualifications only from the standpoint of administration, teacher training, and church goals. Go back now and rate yourself on the scale, one being low and five being high, on these qualities that are important to pupils.

Because these qualities are important to learners, they cannot be overlooked or ignored by teachers. In areas where you are low, work toward improvement with the goal of helping pupils achieve more understanding in learning.

Learning with understanding is not an accident. It requires planning, work, and imagination both by teacher and learners. The teacher, to a large degree, sets the pace for this type of environment. A great deal of effort must be exerted by the teacher. In a monthly newsletter to public-school teachers, a challenge was given at the beginning of a new school year. This same challenge is applicable to teachers who are beginning a new year teaching in a church setting.

"It's a new school year. With new opportunities. And the question before each teacher is simple: to follow the established ways of teaching . . . or to try some new bypaths? And the bypaths most worth exploring are these—new approaches to help students become more independent, more willing learners.

"Many teachers—occupied with traditional methods of teaching —find little opportunity for methods intended to stimulate in students a dedication of learning.

"Still others—equally burdened with instructional duties—will find ways of adding to the standard practices of presentation, review, and testing to enrich and enliven the learning environment. "What makes the difference? It could be a matter of personality. Or imagination. Or interest. But the chances are it's nothing more than just plain good old-fashioned hard work—effort. Effort to bring about change in learning behavior—to guide students in the process of learning—to develop a spirit of inquiry.

"*Effort is output.* It involves the outpouring of your imagination, creativity, intelligence, experience, empathy—all focused on one problem—how to better help children grow emotionally, socially, academically.

"*Effort calls for understanding.* Understanding the nature of the learner. Understanding the nature of the content in relation to the learner. Understanding the need for diversity and the challenge of the teaching act.

"*Effort involves attention to techniques*—Techniques for opening closed minds, for converting indifference to enthusiasm, for capitalizing on diversity in talents and interest, for altering attitudes.

"*Effort involves intensive planning*—

● planning objectives: making yearly plans, semester plans, and short-range plans for unit and daily lessons. And striving for goals that you will be able to measure by what students do and how they behave after your instruction.

● planning methodology: making use of a variety of learning techniques—independent study, group projects, class discussions, differentiated assignments, role playing. Enriching the program through the use of audiovisual aids, field trips, guest speakers.

● planning evaluation: making provisions for determining the effectiveness of your program. Involving students, and sometimes parents, in determining how specific goals are being met."[5]

Molding the lives of boys and girls is an awesome responsibility. Their basic concepts of God and his revelation of himself to man will be determined to a large degree by the opportunities for learning we provide in the church. Resolve to bring about learning with understanding with each pupil you teach.

---

[5] *Teacher's Letter,* Vol. 20, No. 1, Craft Educational Services, Inc. 1970. Used by permission.

CHAPTER SIX
"ROOMS
THAT TEACH"

In walking down the hallway of a church educational building—or a public school, for that matter—have you noticed the differences in rooms? It seems that each room takes on a distinct personality. Some rooms say, "Come in and look around. I'm glad you are here." Other rooms say, "Please don't touch or move an item in the room." At least part of the reason is that a room tends to reflect the personalities of the people who use it, particularly that of the teacher.

Have you ever stopped to analyze the effect that surroundings have upon you? Think back to the last time you entered a softly lighted restuarant. If you were conversing with friends as you entered the room with subdued lighting, you probably lowered your voice almost to a whisper. The head waiter didn't suggest that you talk this way, but the room did!

While shopping for a shirt in a men's store, you look through the carefully stacked shirts, where colors and sizes have been carefully sorted. After making your selection, you put the other shirts in the correct stack. The clerk didn't ask you to, but the way the shirts were displayed did suggest this action. Compare this organized shirt counter to the bargain counter where merchandise is piled high, mixed and jumbled. Soon items are on the floor and prepackaged merchandise is opened. The store management didn't suggest this kind of conduct but the environment did.

The setting of the learning scene is extremely important. It, of course, is secondary to the teacher, the learner, and the curriculum plan. The setting can make learning inviting or it can make it difficult. On the other hand, a multimillion dollar building, ideally built with the best of equipment, doesn't guarantee learning though it can greatly enhance the learning process.

When one shifts from a teacher-centered approach to a learner-centered situation, the physical surroundings change. Hopefully, the day of lined decks or chairs, nailed or screwed to the floors of our public schools is only a part of history.

On the Christian education scene, a shift has been made from the small classroom (approx. 6 by 10 ft.) with one teacher for six to eight pupils to a large room (approx. 25 by 30 ft.) to provide for twenty-five pupils with a team of teachers.

The shift to the department room (sometimes referred to as an "open room") is difficult for some teachers. In fact, it is quite often more difficult for teachers than for the girls and boys. This change in physical facilities began occuring in public education several years back. Even in the public-school, some teachers have difficulty adjusting. Open classrooms often threaten teachers. They fear that it will make control and discipline more difficult. At any time there are several activities or projects that students will be involved in. Some require movement and noise, others the presence of music, and others relative silence and solitude. If the classroom is to resemble life, all of these activities must be permitted to go on simultaneously and not be structured so that some forms of activity are permitted and others (usually the more spontaneous and physical as well as the solitary ones) are not.

The changes in the public-school buildings were started about a decade ago. At first, different school systems experimented by sizing the rooms to fit particular educational uses. However, this seemed only to maintain the traditional stance while varying the size of the classrooms. This was followed by movable partitions which later gave way to the open-school plan. As important as the facilities are, the facilities do not guarantee team teaching and teaching when pupils are greatly involved in the learning process.

Have you ever stopped to analyze the effect of the new trends in public-school education? The open-school plan, through building and space, makes possible a team of teachers working to meet the needs of individuals within the group. It doesn't demand that everyone do the same thing, at the same time, and in the same way.

In a report on the Grant Elementary School in Lakewood, a suburb of Cleveland where there were 125 pupils aged 7 through 9 grouped in instructional units ranging in size from one pupil to 25, the following description was given:

"In one corner, a teacher conducted a traditional class, with 25 students seated at tables. A second teacher presided over a similar group in another corner. In the middle of the room, sprawled on the carpet, was a third teacher and one boy; the lad has special educational problems that require a lot of individual attention, and he was getting it.

"In still another corner, a fourth teacher coached a dozen slow readers. Nearby, behind a piano that offset a small area, 10 pupils sat on the floor around a brightly painted box that contained plug-ins for headsets worn by the children. The box was connected to a small tape machine that played educational cassettes which one of the children had insterted into the machine himself.

"Scattered in other locations about the room were about two dozen children engaged in a variety of self-instruction projects under the eyes of a teacher aide. Some sat at tables, others sat on the carpeted floor, a couple was lying prone, reading books.

"Mrs. Martha Jan McNeill, the principal, pointing out the different levels and types of education going on all at once, remarked: 'The wonderful thing about it is that none of the children knows whether he is in a slow group or a fast group or what, He just knows that they are all in it together.' "[1]

It becomes difficult to separate the method of teaching and the physical facilities because the two go together so completely.

In one further look at public education: "Two educators, who have followed the concept of open education from England to its application in the U. S., sum up its fundamental characteristic as 'openness of self.' Roland Barth and Charles Rathbone put it this way: 'In the open classrooms and in the open school persons are openly sensitive to and supportive of other persons, not closed off by anxiety, threat, custom, and role. Feelings are exposed, acknowledged, and respected, not withheld in fear and defensiveness. Administrators are open to initiatives on the part of teachers; teachers are open to the possibilities inherent in children; children are open to

---

[1] "New Wave in Education—Walls Come Tumbling Down in Open School Plan." *The National Observer.* Nov. 10, 1969, p. 21. Used by permission.

the possibilities inherent in other children, in materials, in themselves.' " [2]

What does all this say to the Christian educator who is concerned about the teaching/learning scene in a church? A great deal has been said about the public schools and their impact upon the church. Regardless of whether or not we subscribe to all the innovations learned about from our school systems, let's remember the boys and girls we teach are greatly influenced and affected by the schools. The pupils' exposure to the public schools in terms of hours is far greater than their exposure to the Christian education program. When Johnny has been given openness and freedom in the learning process and for five days a week employs learning skills in the kind of setting which has been described, are we wise to restrict him and expect him to conform rigidly to a less stimulating environment? The obvious answer is that we want the best for Johnny on the Christian education scene as well as the public-school scene.

Consider the following principles when building new space and providing equipment for the teaching/learning setting.

1. *Good teaching/learning requires involvement of the learner in the learning process. This involvement demands space.* The involvement referred to here goes far beyond "listening" involvement. It is "doing" involvement. Reflect on Chapter 5 where learning with understanding was discussed. Note the various types of learning cited throughout the chapter. In every method illustrated, there was involvement of doing—through investigation, discovering, discussing, role playing, drama, use of art materials, and so forth. Such involvement requires adequate space.

In planning a room, consider twenty-five square feet of floor space per person as a bare minimum. However, if at all possible, plan for twenty-five square feet of free floor space. This means floor space that isn't being used for tables, chairs, bookcases, piano, or other equipment. Because this equipment is needed even if you don't have a maximum enrolment of twenty-five pupils, still consider building a room approximately 25 by 30 feet. For effective involvement and group participation maximum enrolment should be limited to twenty-five which may suggest your building a room 25 by 35 feet. A rec-

---

[2] *Teacher's Letter,* Vol. 19, No. 5, Craft Educational Services, Inc. 1969. Used by permission.

tangular room lends itself better to a good teaching situation. If possible, build the room with a width-length ratio of two to three. Windows should be placed on the long side of the room, 24 to 30 inches from the floor.

2. *Participation from the learner is best achieved in an informal setting.* The room can very easily set the mood for or against participation. Group tables within the room in such a way that pupils will be encouraged to participate in the large-group experiences. For example, the tables may be arranged as in the sketch below if pupils are to remain at the tables during the large group.

If the lead teacher prefers the smaller groups to merge and become one large group, individuals may move their chairs to form a semicircle. (This procedure is particularly desirable with the younger grades.) Tables may be moved back to allow more room for the semicircle as shown in the sketch below:

In either situation, both teachers and learners should be drawn into the large group. The teachers certainly would not stand at the back of the room and watch or sit behind the semicircle. Instead, if the small groups remain at their tables, each teacher stays with his group at their table. Or if the small groups merge, each teacher joins the large group in the semicircle and sits within the circle. (The wise teacher will know if there are two pupils that need to be separated in the large group, or which one needs a teacher nearby.)

Preferably the lead teacher will conduct the large group while seated—assuming he can maintain good eye contact with each pupil in the room.

Placing the chairs in rows kills the informality being strived for. Therefore this type of arrangement in the room is discouraged.

3. *Furnishings and equipment should be geared to the pupils.* Boys and girls of elementary age have unique needs that can be met through utilization of the right kinds of furnishings. Chair and table heights become important only if they are wrong. The following chart may be used to check the dimensions on chairs and tables which become the basic equipment for your department.

Grade of child	Chair seat from floor	Table height from floor
First Grade	12	22

Second Grade	12	22
Third Grade	14	24
Fourth Grade	14	24
Fifth Grade	16	26
Sixth Grade	16	26

Tables should be large enough for six to eight pupils to work comfortably around. Thirty by forty-eight is a good size tabletop. If possible, the tabletops should be a water-resistant material that can be easily cleaned. Then when the table is used for painting, modeling of clay or other materials, the making of relief maps, and similar activities, the tabletop will not require special care or attention.

Small groups are highly mobile and will, of necessity, move chairs from time to time. Therefore, the chairs should be lightweight but sturdy. The less bulky chair takes less room and is therefore more desirable.

On an interior wall of the room, consider cabinets with Masonite counter top at the child's level (28 in. from the floor) with sink and running water. Overhead hanging wall cabinets are ideal for storage of seasonal materials, books, and other resources not directly related to the current unit of study.

4. *Resource materials, learning aids, and supplies should be readily available to the pupils.* The room, equipment, and furnishings should all serve as appetizers to learning for the pupils. A resource center for each room should become the hub for the learning activities. Books, recordings, Bibles, commetaries, Bible atlases, missionary biographies, dictionaries, and maps are some of the basics for a resource center. In selecting these materials, the abilities and learning skills of the learner will have to determine the kinds and the degree of complexity. For instance in a department for first and second graders, the books should consist mainly of pictorial content. More recordings and visuals will be used because the children cannot read with the skill that fifth or sixth graders can. However in a depart-

ment for sixth graders, many of the resource items will require reading skills and research skills.

Nearby open shelves should be well stocked with supplies needed in the learning projects. The child is free to draw from the supplies and from the resource center. Because of the freedom and flow of work within the department room, all of the small groups can use the same resource center and supplies. When such materials as these are available and accessible to the pupil, he will often take initiative in going far beyond the prescribed boundaries of a learning project. The room that teaches certainly encourages further exploration and learning.

5. *Involvement of all the senses should be planned for when constructing space.* Because children learn through all five of the senses (seeing, hearing, touching, smelling, and tasting), plan space that can utilize all of these. Some considerations to keep in mind when building are these:

(1) Construct rooms that can be darkened easily. Films, filmstrips, and slides offer wonderful opportunities for teaching. Boys and girls may not be able to visit a mission field in person, but they can learn a great deal about the people from a faraway land, their customs, and beliefs, and the work of missionaries through films and filmstrips. This same idea can be used even through the viewing of slides made by a missionary. In planning the room, consider where the projector will be and blank (white) wall space for the showing of the pictures.

(2) Provide a sufficient number of electrical outlets. Many opportunities for learning require electricity. The projector just mentioned needs power. The record player or tape recorder offers many opportunities for exploration and learning. In a nature unit a small group could pop corn and explore one of God's wonders. All of these experiences are dependent upon a well-planned room.

(3) Plan a sink with running water in the room. Many art materials require water. Having it in the room will encourage the otherwise hesitant teacher to utilize this media of teaching. The restroom can be down the hall and still suffice; however, a sink in the room is highly desirable.

(4) Plan windows that are low enough for the group to view outside scenery. Even if the view overlooks rooftops, a beautiful rainbow can be enjoyed or a sunset. The changing of the seasons,

the falling of snow or rain provides excellent conversation starters for teaching about God.

6. *Because learning will occur more easily when pupils are comfortable, ventilation and lighting should be carefully planned.* A hot, stuffy room suggests taking a nap or sluggishness. The room with not enough heat will cause the pupil's mind to think, How can I get warm enough? rather than to think in the area of the unit of study. When properly planned and utilized, a room calls no attention to itself but provides an excellent atmosphere for learning.

In colder areas, heat should be turned on early enough to have the room comfortable by the arrival of the first pupil; in warmer climates, air-conditioning should play the same role.

If possible, plan the large group experiences to face an interior wall with pupils' backs to the windows. Making children face the bright sun or a glare can in itself cause discipline problems.

Openness and freedom encourage inquiry, exploration, and learning. Buildings should provide this environment. Therefore, in planning a building, consider only the one room—the open-school plan—for any department involving children from grades one through six. Plan at least twenty-five square feet of free floor space per person enrolled.

Carpeting in elementary departments helps to create a relaxed, informal atmosphere. Carpeting absorbs noise and will, therefore, help create a quieter department. Quite often, the boys and girls will sit on the floor to work.

But We Can't Build!

So far in this chapter we have discussed building the ideal room. Only the highly desirable aspects were listed. Now what about the church that is stuck for the next 20 years with a building already obsolete? Is team teaching dependent upon the department room (open room) approach?

Good teaching can take place in less than desirable facilities. Perhaps the most common provision in the past has been an assembly room with small classrooms grouped around it. Therefore, your facilities may look something like that shown on the following pages.

Now by taking these three steps, you can move toward better use of your facilities, remembering that facilities do not guarantee good teaching. (Good teaching is up to you—the teacher).

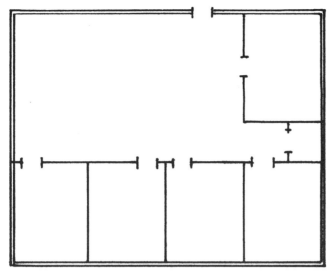

1. *Remove all unnecessary equipment from the department. All the floor space needs to be utilized for the entire teaching period.*

The traditional approach of assembly period-classroom work segmented the teaching and the floor space. All of the pupils were "rowed-up" in the assembly area for a period and then all the pupils were put in tiny classrooms, six to ten per room. This necessitated a dual set of equipment or at least of chairs.

The idea of total-period teaching requires total use of the space. Therefore, each pupil does not need two chairs—but only one. Each pupil does need the additional floor space being used by that extra chair. So one of the first steps is to eliminate the extra set of chairs that is now in the assembly area. This will likely free up to one half of your present floor space that can be used for teaching during the entire teaching period. With the chairs removed, place one or two of your small groups (depending on the size of the assembly area) in the large room.

If there are folding doors between any two of the small rooms, open these—or better still remove them. Place the remaining small groups in the largest classrooms available.

Placing one or two small groups in the assembly area will eliminate their having to move when it is time for the large group. Only the groups in the small classrooms will need to bring their chairs and assemble for the large-group teaching experience.

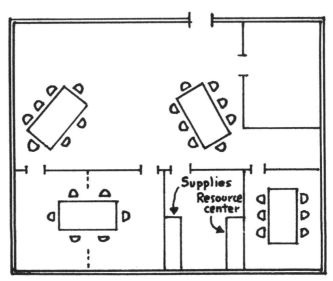

By making this shift in your present space, your department may look like that shown above.

2. *Remove doors that open to the assembly area from the small classrooms.*

As has been stated earlier, there needs to be an openness and freedom within the department that closed doors deter. A flow of work from the small group into the large group is made possible when doors are taken down. The lead teacher will see and know of all the learning projects occuring in the small groups. Pupils will be free to leave the small groups and go to the resource center to get a book, dictionary, or other learning aid. Quite often during the evolvement of a learning project, additional materials are needed. The pupil is free to obtain these supplies from the open shelves nearby.

Pins from the hinges on the doors may be removed with little effort and doors can be stored. (If your church cannot afford tables for each small group, attach legs to the doors, making tables. The doornob can be removed and the hole filled with plastic wood or putty.)

3. *Establish a resource and supplies center for the department.*

The next step you need to take is to establish a resource and supplies center for the department. This may be placed in a corner of the large room; or if you have a small classroom not now used, it can be your resource and supplies area. Open shelves and a bookcase are good to have; however, the resource and supplies may be stored in boxes labeled for each category of items.

Essentials for the resource center are: Bible dictionary, Bible atlas, concordance, one-volume commentary, modern speech versions of the Bible, picture books of Bible lands, missionary biographies and other selected books on the reading level of the pupils. (Consult your curriculum materials for books to use to enrich each unit. These books may be checked out of your church library or a public library.)

Supplies needed for each department include:

newsprint (18 by 24 inches or larger)
writing paper (8½ by 11 or 9 by 12)
rolled paper (28 or 30 inches wide)
crayons
colored chalk
felt-tip pins
pencils
tempera paint
brushes for painting
remnants of cloth (for costumes)
yarn/string
paper bags
glue/cement
stapler/staples
index cards

(Consult your curriculum materials for supplies needed for each unit. The items listed above are basic for most units.)

In summary, there is little, if any, justification for continuing to build assembly rooms and classrooms for use by pupils in the elementary grades (grades 1–6). This statement is made because:

1. Lower enrolment (maximum of 25 pupils) offsets the need for partitions between classes.

2. Today's children are accustomed to working in small groups within the classroom and are not distracted by what is taking place at other places in the room.

3. A department without classrooms encourages improved teaching by (1) giving the lead teacher opportunity to more closely observe the teaching/learning which is taking place in each of the small groups; (2) making it possible for the lead teacher to lend support quickly to any teacher as difficulties arise; (3) making pos-

sible more flexibility in grouping pupils for special purposes; (4) making accessible to each small group all of the resources available to the department, such as record player or art materials.

The physical facility does make a big impact on the teaching/learning. Even though it doesn't guarantee good learning, it can easily create an environment for exploration and searching. Plan for your room to say to the pupil, "Come in. I'm here to help you learn. Use every facet of me as you search for truth!"

CHAPTER SEVEN
"OVERCOMING
OBSTACLES"

How does one move from the familiar—the comfortable—to the unfamiliar—the strange? Change is very difficult and the older we get, the more difficult change becomes for most of us. The entire book has been contrasting the traditional approach to teaching (in a Christian education setting) to team with a heavy emphasis on involvement and participation of the learner.

There are two big questions now that you must deal with. The first is how you—one teacher—can make this transtion in your role as a Christian educator. You may have already overcome the obstacles. Hopefully, if you have read the preceding chapters of the book, you will have seen the value in teaching with more involvement and participaton. If so, the second question deals with the other members of the teaching team (those who work in the department with you). How can you lead others with whom you teach to accept change?

Before change for the better can be experienced by a teaching team, the team must share a common attitude concerning the value of learning. Anything that is worthwhile comes at a price. Meaningful learning can only be achieved at price, and the price may be costly in terms of time, preparation, and willingness to change and grow on the part of the teacher. Until a teacher sees his task or role in Christian education as one of extreme importance and high priority, he will not be willing to pay the high price. His dedication to the job as teacher and his sense of call from God to teach are foundational in overcoming obstacles. Once these two are right, you can be educated to change. However one's dedication to God and sense of calling must be experiential and not educational. These two result from a personal encounter with God. They do not come about only through intellectual understanding.

One's general attitude toward teaching greatly affects the way he teaches. As a member of a teaching team, you will place more emphasis on learning than on teaching. Your first consideration will be on the learner and what is happening to him and what he is experiencing rather than on the teacher and what the teacher is doing. Giving attention first to the learner determines the work of the teacher. By placing more emphasis on learning, you will continually check yourself on the involvement of the learner, checking to determine that he is more than a passive listener, more than one who is sitting still—he may not even be listening.

How can you rate the involvement of the pupils in the learning experiences you are guiding for them? As the unit of study is being planned, be aware that learning takes place through all of the senses—seeing, hearing, touching, smelling, and tasting. And the more senses that are used in a given session, the greater degree of involvement and learning takes place.

The first three senses are the ones to check more closely, but do not rule out smelling and tasting. The Bible story of Mary pouring costly perfume on Jesus because of her love and devotion to him was greatly enhanced with a group of third graders when they smelled the fragrance from a newly opened bottle of expensive perfume and heard the Bible story. A unit entitled "Life in the Days of Jesus" made an indelible impression on second graders when each one tasted such foods as cheese, grapes, raisins, figs, olives, and dates and were reminded that these were the kinds of foods eaten by Jesus. The following list indicates some learning projects and experiences that involve different senses. As you study the list carefully, note the learning projects that involve more than one sense. As a rule these are the more desirable learning experiences because these projects open the way to a higher degree of involvement and participation by the learners. (For a full description of most of the learning projects, see *Guiding Children* by Rives and Sharp, Convention Press, Nashville, 1969.)

Hearing

Bible verse games
block printing
books
box puppets
brainstorming
buzz groups
case study
choral speaking
creating songs
creative writing
curios
discussion
dramatization
face-mask puppets
fact games
field trip
films
filmstrips
flash card games
flip chart
finish it

formal games
free association quiz
interview
learning hymns
lecture-forum
letterwriting
listening teams
litany
map study
marionettes
match-the-halves
   game
match-the-word game
monologue
music
musical instruments
newspaper puppets
newspaper writing
painting
panel-forum
paper-bag puppets

papier-mâché pup-
   pets
poems
printmaking
problem solving
puppets
questions and an-
   swers
quiz games
research
review games
role playing
singing
skill games
stick puppets
stocking puppets
storywriting
strategy games
symposium-forum
tabletop scenes
time lines

Seeing

Bible verse games
block printing

blueprinting
books

box puppets
cartooning

case study
charts
clay modeling
collage
creating songs
creative writing
curios
diorama
dramatization
drawing
face-mask puppets
fact games
field trips
fill-in-the-blank
films
filmstrips
finger painting
finish it
flash card game
flat map
flip chart
floor scenes
formal games
free association quiz

frieze
globe
interview
learning hymns
map study
marionettes
match-the-halves
   game
match-the-word game
mobiles
modeling
models
montage
mosaic
mural
musical instruments
newspaper puppets
newspaper writing
painting
panorama
pantomime
paper-bag puppets
paper cutting
paper tearing

paper-mask puppets
peep box
photography
picture posing
pictures
poems
posters
printmaking
puppets
quiz games
relief map
research
review games
role playing
scenes
skill games
spatter painting
stick puppets
stocking puppets
storywriting
strategy game
tabletop scenes
time lines
writing

Touching

Bible verse games
block printing
blueprinting
books
box puppets
cartooning
charts
clay modeling
collage
creative songs
creative writing
curios

diorama
dramatization
drawing
face-mask puppets
fact games
field trip
fill-in-the-blank
finger painting
finish it
flash card game
flat maps
flip chart

floor game
formal games
free association quiz
frieze
globes
learning hymns
map study
marionettes
match-the-halves
   games
match-the-word
   games

mobiles	painting	posters
modeling	panorama	quiz games
models	pantomime	relief map
montage	paper-bag puppets	review games
mosaic	paper cutting	scenes
mural	paper tearing	skill games
musical instruments	peep boxes	stick puppets
newspaper puppets	picture posing	string painting
newspaper writing		

Smelling

field trips

Tasting

field trips

Now after you have analyzed your teaching by determining the senses involved, look at some broad categories of learning projects. In each unit of study, there should be balance among the types of learning experiences. (Each of these can involve at least three of the senses). Use a work sheet similar to the one below and list (write in) the learning projects for your next unit of study. Perhaps it will point up some areas of weakness, omission or duplication.

Category	Learning Projects
Art	
Books	
Creative Writing	

Displays (models)

Drama

Group Vocals

Interviewing

Learning Games/Puzzles

Music

Map Study

Nature

Projected Visual Aids

Research

Participation and involvement of the learner aids him not only in hearing about concepts but in visualizing and even dramatizing concepts. The learner has opportunity for "instant replay" where he can test his concept of a new or different idea. The entire group (either small group or large group) becomes the reactor and consequently each learner is testing or trying out the concept or idea he is beginning to grasp. (This grasping is often referred to as internalization.)

Now let's deal with the second big question that was introduced at the beginning of the chapter. We will assume that you—one member of the department—are convinced that team teaching with a heavy emphasis on involvement and participation of the learner is a better way to teach than the approaches now used in your department. How can you help the other teaching members of your department overcome the obstacles and move to an improved way of teaching/learning?

Change cannot be legislated. The desire to change must come from within the individual. Bringing about change in a group of teachers who serve on a volunteer basis is often more difficult than implementing change in public education where teachers are professionally trained and are paid for their services. Now, how can you as one person bring about this change in your department?

1. *Create an attitude of trust and respect among the teachers.* Your attitude will probably be your greatest asset or biggest hinderance in bringing about change. Patience and understanding are two essential ingredients in a good attitude. The innovative teacher must convey the idea that his innovations or changes are desired not for his own glory but for the benefit of those whom he teaches.

The teaching team (the persons) are more important than any

method or set of methodologies. As this fact is realized, there will be a higher degree of respect and trust among the teachers in the department. A willingness and desire to change requires a high degree of maturity. A mature person does respect and trust others.

2. *Strengthen bonds of Christian fellowship.* Much has been written and said on the subject of Christian fellowship, and yet it is an idea or concept hard to adequately verbalize. A group of persons with similar life goals and a life-changing experience have a great deal in common. From this base, meaningful personal Christian relationships grow. In some groups of Christian leaders, this growth is almost instantaneous; in other groups it comes more slowly. However, in all groups who are Christian, there is the potential for this Christian fellowship. When trust and mutual respect are present, it comes immediately. Christian fellowship can be cultivated in your department among the teachers.

3. *Employ the principles and methods discussed in this book with the group (class) you teach.* Even though the teachers in your department are not team teaching, you can use the principles discussed in Chapter 1 and the approaches illustrated in Chapter 5 as you teach your group. The learners in your group will become more involved and will be participating to a greater degree. Their enthusiasm will be evident. Meaningful experiences of the pupils in your class will be spontaneously shared with others. Without your pressing the point, the other teachers in the department will begin to inquire how you do it. Hence the door of change will begin to open.

In one fourth-grade department using the traditional approach to teaching, Mrs. Ketner was enlisted as a new teacher. As an insightful person in the teaching/learning process, she began to involve her group in unit planning. Pupils were respected as persons and made decisions concerning the project on which they would work. Learning games and puzzles were used to supplement the other work planned by the group. What had been a passive, unexciting, and unexcited group of boys and girls suddenly came alive! There was interest and enthusiasm in Bible teaching. Other teachers in the department noticed this change and began asking such questions as, "How do you do it?" The door was opened and the whole department moved toward improved teaching.

4. *Involve a "third party" if conflict seems to arise.* Sometimes a new idea is more easily and quickly accepted if it is presented by an

"expert" (someone from outside the department). Bringing in a third party (an outsider) often is a successful way to manage conflict. This may be a person from your church but from outside the department who can fill this role. However, if there is no one in your church with the background for and understanding of team teaching, go outside to find help. Several denominations have personnel employed to assist churches. These persons are skilled in managing conflict and in selling an idea. Qualified personnel from another church may be secured and brought in for consultation and help.

These four broad ideas are directed at helping you initiate change in your department. These ideas need to be implemented with tact and patience. Acceptance of the idea will come more quickly in some departments than in others. If an idea is accepted by the teachers or not, continue this improved teaching approach in the group (class) for which you are responsible. Example is the greatest teacher. And because we are teaching boys and girls religious concepts, we have a responsibility for teaching the best way we know.

5. *Ask for, seek out, and participate in training.* When the concept of team teaching is accepted, move quickly to train. Any job that is worth doing is worth training for and teaching jobs in the church are no exception. Training to be a good teacher is a continual process. Better and more effective ways of communicating are constantly being discovered and need to be incorporated into the program of Christian education.

One way every teacher can be trained is through a personal reading/study program. This is possible even in the smallest church where study groups are not formed. The curriculum materials along with the Bible become the basic sources for a personal study program.

The base of all Christian education rests on the Bible. Yet many who teach are biblically illiterate. Every teacher should have a program of in-depth Bible study. Choose one book of the Bible at a time and make a thorough study of it; or choose a Bible personality and learn all you can about how God used this individual. Some excellent guidance is given for an individual Bible study plan in the inexpensive leaflet *Guidelines for Bible Study for Workers with Preschoolers and Children* by Jester Summers.[1]

---

[1] Jester Summers, *Guidelines for Bible Study for Workers with Preschoolers and Children.* Church Literature Department, 127 Ninth Avenue North, Nashville, Tennessee.

Another area a teacher needs help in is with developmental needs of the learner, methodology of teaching and learning, and the administration of Christian education. Various denominations offer study books on these subjects at a nominal cost.

Books from the field of professional elementary education provide another area for personal reading and study. A visit to the church and public libraries will help you survey the books and magazines available in your community. Set a goal of reading certain ones during the coming year. Through a plan of personal reading (study) you will grow and experience training in your task of teaching.

Study sessions offer another opportunity for training. For instance, the workers in your department can participate in study sessions where this book, for example, could be used as a basis for group study. A study leader or teacher may be designated to lead the group in the study. Many churches offer study courses in which various books designed to train teachers and other church members are studied. These study sessions may be part of a number of courses offered simultaneously or in series by the church. Or a special study may be initiated by your department alone.

Participation in some community projects can also aid in training workers. For individuals fortunate enough to reside in a college or university city or town, there will be many opportunities to hear guest lecturers speak on subjects related to the education of children. From time to time Parent-Teacher Associations plan programs of information and interpretation on the child as a learner. Children's museums may also sponsor projects that are informative to the persons interested in childhood education.

Observation in a department where boys and girls are being taught well is one of the best means of leadership training. When teachers who are hesitant about making changes can observe in a department where meaningful learning is occuring, acceptance of change comes more easily. How does one go about observing?

First, locate a department where desirable teaching/learning is taking place. Secure approval from the lead teacher for you (and possibly two or three of your teachers) to observe during a teaching session. The first session of unit of study is a good time to observe. Ask to meet with the teachers you will observe prior to the observation. Look at the room; ask questions about schedules and plans.

Some guidelines for you to follow as you observe in another department are:

—Arrive early and sit in the room where you will be least noticed and out of the way.

—Do not wear clothes or jewelry that will call attention to yourself.

—Do not participate in the session—merely sit quietly and observe.

—Analyze (in your mind) the strengths and weaknesses of the teaching going on.

—Make brief notes or questions on subjects where you want to follow up after the session.

—Evaluate the involvement and participation of the learners.

—Determine if the session is teacher centered or pupil centered.

—Note strengths and weaknesses of both large and small groups.

—Observe how problems and difficulties are handled.

If at all possible, meet with the teachers you observe at their next planning meeting at which time you can ask additional questions. If this isn't feasible, plan for an immediate chat with the local teacher following the observation.

Approach observation with the idea of *your* learning from it. Workers you observe will be more willing for you to see them and their mistakes if your attitude is one of learning and not one of criticism.

As you and the workers in your department overcome the obstacles and move to more creative teaching, be willing for teachers from other departments to observe in your department. Observation is also an excellent way to introduce a prospective teacher to team teaching. Parents who express interest in their child's work at church may be invited to observe.

There are so many advantages to observation, that some churches build observation booths adjacent to an elementary department. These booths can be entered from outside the department room and observers can see the learning environment in action without the boys and girls seeing the observers. These booths provide the setting for a continual teacher-training and parent-education program.

When observation booths are built, one way glass or $\frac{1}{16}$ inch mesh screen can be used. The mesh screen is less expensive and does not require microphones in the room. The screen should be installed diagonally with the viewing area above the eye level of the children being observed. The floor of the booths should be raised higher (18″ to 24″) than the floor where the boys and girls are. The inside of the booth should be painted a dark color. When dark clothes are worn by the observers, the boys and girls will not see persons in the booth. For additional suggestions on how to construct observation booths, read pages 370–371 of *Infant and Child in the Culture of Today*.[2]

Of necessity, the book has been divided into chapters. These chapters have dealt with important aspects of teaching the child . . . the goals and objectives . . . the child as a learner . . . the teacher as a guide for the learning process . . . the teachers forming a team . . . the planning process . . . the rooms in which the teaching/learning occurs, and finally a challenge for teachers to move toward new dimensions in teaching children. As you reflect on the book, hopefully you do not see seven isolated segments (chapters) but a blending that will speak to a sound philosophy of teaching boys and girls. All persons related to the child (teacher, parent, church,) want the best for him. The following quote from *Business Condition Weekly* published by the Alexander Hamilton Institute undergirds this philosophy as it speaks of the public-school.

Parents are no longer satisfied by children who can recite the answers to questions because they have memorized the expected answer. More parents want their children to understand, to be able to deal with concepts rather than to repeat answers by rote.

In other words, more people are accepting the idea that the learning process is one in which the child must be vitally involved. This means that the classroom, ideally, is no longer the place where the teacher dictates from a fixed spot in front of the blackboard to a rigid group of seated children who have been drained of all spontaneity and curiosity.

One of the most successful new child-centered learning approaches which does away with the traditional teacher-oriented classroom in elementary schools is the "Open Classroom." This is actually an adaptation of methods referred to as "British Infant School," Leicestershire Method," "Integrated Days," and "Open Corridor."

---

[2] Arnold Gesell and Frances Ilg, *Infant and Child in the Culture of Today.* Harper and Brothers Publishers, New York, © 1943.

Since World War II, the method has been widely and successfully used in the British school system. In the past five years, it has been introduced to many American schools including such disparate classrooms as those of rural Vermont and North Dakota and the urban, inner-city schools of Boston, New York, Washington, and Philadelphia.

The most basic principles of the Open Classroom are complete respect for and trust in the child, and an underlying belief that each child is an individual who wants to learn and that each child will learn in his or her own way. When these principles are applied, the classroom becomes a place of excitement and stimulation.

The Open Classroom is characterized by its emphasis on learning rather than teaching; on the individual child's thinking processes and problem-solving abilities; and on the freedom and responsibility given to each child.[3]

[3] *Business Conditions Weekly,* Personal Management Section, Vol. XLVII No. 32, August 17, 1970, Part Two, page 1. Copyright © 1970 by Alexander Hamilton Institute, Inc. All rights reserved. Used by permission.

APPENDIX

The following Bible verses have been selected for use with elementary-age children. These may be used to supplement units of study or in preparation of learning games and puzzles. This is by no means a comprehensive or exhaustive listing but does give a broad range of verses that may be used as teaching enrichment. The verses are grouped by categories.

BIBLE

All scripture is given by inspiration of God. 2 Timothy 3:16
All that the Lord hath said will we do, and be obedient. Exodus 24:7
All my commandments are truth. Psalm 119:151
And God spake all these words. Exodus 20:1
Be ye doers of the word, and not hearers only. James 1:22
Blessed are they that hear the word of God, and keep it. Luke 11:28
Blessed be the Lord . . . there hath not failed one word of all his good promise. 1 Kings 8:56
Go ye into all the world, and preach the gospel. Mark 16:15
Hear ye the word of the Lord. Jeremiah 2:4
He that keepeth the law, happy is he. Proverbs 29:18
If ye love me, keep my commandments. John 14:15
I will instruct thee and teach thee in the way which thou shalt go. Psalm 32:8
I will not forget thy word. Psalm 119:16
Lead me in thy truth, and teach me. Psalm 25:5
These things write we unto you, that your joy may be full. 1 John 1:4
These are written, that ye might believe that Jesus is the Christ, the Son of God. John 20:31
Thou art near, O Lord; and all thy commandments are truth. Psalm 119:151
Thy word is true from the beginning. Psalm 119:160

CHOICES

A friend loveth at all times. Proverbs 17:17

All that the Lord hath said will we do, and be obedient. Exodus 24:7

And this is his commandment, That we . . . love one another. 1 John 3:23

A soft answer turneth away wrath. Proverbs 15:1

As ye would that men should do to you, do ye also to them. Luke 6:31

A wise son heareth his father's instruction. Proverbs 13:1

Blessed are they that hear the word of God, and keep it. Luke 11:28

Call upon me in the day of trouble. Psalm 50:15

Cease to do evil; learn to do well. Isaiah 1:16–17

Children, obey your parents. Ephesians 6:1

Children, obey your parents. Colossians 3:20

Do all things without murmurings and disputings. Philippians 2:14

Do for others just what you want them to do for you. Luke 6:31, TEV

Do that which is honest. 2 Corinthians 13:7

Do those things that are pleasing in [God's] his sight. 1 John 3:22

Have peace one with another. Mark 9:50

I do always those things that please him. John 8:29

If ye love me, keep my commandments. John 14:15

I will behave myself wisely. Psalm 101:2

Learn to do well. Isaiah 1:17

Let us not love in word, . . . but in deed. 1 John 3:18

Lie not one to another. Colossians 3:9

Love your enemies, bless them that curse you, do good to them that hate you, and pray for them which despitefully use you, and persecute you. Matthew 5:44

My mouth shall speak truth. Proverbs 8:7

Refuse the evil, and choose the good. Isaiah 7:15

Speak every man truth with his neighbour. Ephesians 4:25

Speak not evil one of another. James 4:11

Thou shalt not steal. Exodus 20:15

Thou shalt do that which is right and good in the sight of the Lord. Deuteronomy 6:18

Teach me to do thy will. Psalm 143:10

Treat men exactly as you would like them to treat you. Luke 6:31, Phillips

We . . . do those things that are pleasing in his sight. 1 John 3:22

We know that all things work together for good to them that love God. Romans 8:28

We ought to obey God rather than men. Acts 5:29

Whatsoever ye do in word or deed, do all in the name of the Lord Jesus. Colossians 3:17

Whatsoever ye would that men should do to you, do ye even so to them. Matthew 7:12

Ye are my friends, if ye do whatsoever I command you. John 15:14

CHURCH

And he commanded us to preach unto the people, and to testify. Acts 10:42

As his custom was, he [Jesus] went into the synagogue on the sabbath day. Luke 4:16

Bring an offering, and come before him: worship the Lord in the beauty of holiness. 1 Chronicles 16:29

Christ . . . loved the church, and gave himself for it. Ephesians 5:25

Enter into his gates with thanksgiving, and into his courts with praise. Psalm 100:4

Every man shall give as he is able, according to the blessing of the Lord. Deuteronomy 16:17

For we preach not ourselves, but Christ Jesus the Lord; and ourselves your servants for Jesus' sake. 2 Corinthians 4:5

Give unto the Lord the glory due unto his name: bring an offering, and come into his courts, O worship the Lord in the beauty of holiness. Psalm 96:8–9

God hath set some in the church, first apostles, secondarily prophets, thirdly teachers. 1 Corinthians 12:28

It is a good thing to give thanks unto the Lord, and to sing praises unto thy name, O most High. Psalm 92:1

I was glad when they said unto me, Let us go into the house of the Lord. Psalm 122:1

I will be glad and rejoice in thee: I will sing praise to thy name, O thou most High. Psalm 9:2

I will give thanks unto thee, O Lord, . . . I will sing praises unto thy name. 2 Samuel 22:50

I will hear what God the Lord will speak. Psalm 85:8
I will praise the name of God with a song. Psalm 69:30
Men ought always to pray. Luke 18:1
My house shall be called the house of prayer. Matthew 21:13
The Lord is in his holy temple: let all the earth keep silence before him. Habakkuk 2:20
When thou goest to the house of God, . . . be more ready to hear. Ecclesiastes 5:1

GOD

All that the Lord hath said will we do, and be obedient. Exodus 24:7
All things were made by him; and without him was not anything made that was made. John 1:3
Behold, God is mine helper. Psalm 54:4
Be not afraid, . . . for the Lord thy God is with thee. Joshua 1:9
Blessed are the peacemakers: for they shall be called the children of God. Matthew 5:9
Blessed be the Lord . . . there hath not failed one word of all his good promise. 1 Kings 8:56
Every good gift and every perfect gift is from above, and cometh down from the father. James 1:17
Every man should eat and drink, . . . it is the gift of God. Ecclesiastes 3:13
For we are labourers together with God. 1 Corinthians 3:9
Give unto the Lord the glory due unto his name: bring an offering, and come into his courts, O worship the Lord in the beauty of holiness. Psalm 96:8–9.
God created man. Genesis 1:27
God . . . giveth us richly all things to enjoy. 1 Timothy 6:17
[God] hath made of one blood all nations of men for to dwell on the face of the earth. Acts 17:26
God is love. 1 John 4:8
God is our refuge and strength, a very present help in trouble. Psalm 46:1
God . . . loved us, and sent his Son. 1 John 4:10
God loveth a cheerful giver. 2 Corinthians 9:7
God saw every thing that he had made, and, behold, it was very good. Genesis 1:31
God shall supply all your need. Philippians 4:19

God so loved the world, that he gave his only begotten son, that whosoever believeth in him should not perish, but have everlasting life. John 3:16

God treats all men alike. Acts 10:34, TEV

Great is the Lord, and greatly to be praised. Psalm 145:3

Have we not all one father? hath not one God created us? Malachi 2:10

Hear, O Israel: The Lord our God is one Lord: and thou shalt love the Lord thy God with all thine heart, and with all thy soul, and with all thy might. Deuteronomy 6:4–5

In the beginning God created the heaven and the earth. Genesis 1:1

In wisdom hast thou made them all. Psalm 104:24

I will hear what God the Lord will speak. Psalm 85:8

I will instruct thee and teach thee in the way which thou shalt go. Psalm 32:8

Know ye that the Lord he is God: it is he that hath made us, and not we ourselves. Psalm 100:3

Lord, be thou my helper. Psalm 30:10

Many, O Lord my God, are thy wonderful works which thou hast done. Psalm 40:5

Oh that men would praise the Lord for his goodness, and for his wonderful works to the children of men! Psalm 107:31

O give thanks unto the Lord, for he is good. Psalm 107:1

O Lord, how great are thy works! and thy thoughts are very deep. Psalm 92:5

O Lord, how manifold are thy works! in wisdom hast thou made them all: the earth is full of thy riches. Psalm 104:24

O sing unto the Lord a new song; for he hath done marvellous things. Psalm 98:1

The Lord hath been mindful of us. Psalm 115:12

The Lord he is God: it is he that hath made us. Psalm 100:3

The Lord is good. Nahum 1:7

The Lord is nigh unto all them that call upon him. Psalm 145:18

The Lord is the strength of my life; of whom shall I be afraid? Psalm 27:1

The Lord is the true God. Jeremiah 10:10

The Lord shall give that which is good. Psalm 85:12

The Lord thy God . . . doth go with thee. Deuteronomy 31:6

The word of our God shall stand for ever. Isaiah 40:8

[God said] The world is mine. Psalm 50:12

Thou, Lord, art good, and ready to forgive. Psalm 86:5

Thou, Lord, hast made me glad through thy work. Psalm 92:4

Truly God is good. Psalm 73:1

Thy lovingkindness is good. Psalm 69:16

We have thought of thy lovingkindness, O God, in the midst of thy temple. Psalm 48:9

GOD'S CARE

Be not afraid, . . . for the Lord thy God is with thee. Joshua 1:9

Blessed be the Lord . . . there hath not failed one word of all his good promise. 1 Kings 8:56

Call upon me in the day of trouble. Psalm 50:15

Every good gift and every perfect gift is from above, and cometh down from the father. James 1:17

Freely ye have received, freely give. Matthew 10:8

God . . . giveth us richly all things to enjoy. 1 Timothy 6:17

God is our refuge and strength, a very present help in trouble. Psalm 46:1

God saw every thing that he had made, and, behold, it was very good. Genesis 1:31

God shall supply all your need. Philippians 4:19

Go home to thy friends, and tell them how great things the Lord hath done for thee. Mark 5:19

He careth for you. 1 Peter 5:7

He causeth the grass to grow for the cattle, and herb for the service of man: that he may bring forth food out of the earth. Psalm 104:14

He [God] maketh the storm a calm, so that the waves thereof are still. Psalm 107:29

[God says] I am with thee, and will keep thee in all places whither thou goest. Genesis 28:15

I will fear no evil: for thou art with me. Psalm 23:4

[God says] I will not fail thee, nor forsake thee. Joshua 1:5

I will trust, and not be afraid. Isaiah 12:2

[Jesus said] Lo, I am with you alway. Matthew 28:20

O give thanks unto the Lord, . . . who giveth food to all. Psalm 136:1,25

O Lord, how manifold are thy works! in wisdom hast thou made them all: the earth is full of thy riches. Psalm 104:24

O Lord my God, in thee do I put my trust. Psalm 7:1

Praise ye the Lord . . . which giveth food to the hungry. Psalm 146:1,7

Rejoice in every good thing which the Lord thy God hath given unto thee. Deuteronomy 26:11

The Lord hath been mindful of us. Psalm 115:12

The Lord hath done great things for us; whereof we are glad. Psalm 126:3

The Lord is good to all: and his tender mercies are over all his works. All thy works shall praise thee, O Lord. Psalm 145:9–10

The Lord is my helper, and I will not fear. Hebrews 13:6

The Lord is nigh unto all them that call upon him. Psalm 145:18

The Lord is the strength of my life; of whom shall I be afraid? Psalm 27:1

The Lord thy God is with thee. Joshua 1:9

The Lord will hear when I call unto him. Psalm 4:3

There hath not failed one word of all his good promise. 1 Kings 8:56

Thou art my help. Psalm 40:17

What time I am afraid, I will trust in thee. Psalm 56:3

While the earth remaineth, seedtime and harvest, and cold and heat, and summer and winter, and day and night shall not cease. Genesis 8:22

HOME

A wise son heareth his father's instruction. Proverbs 13:1

Be not forgetful to entertain strangers. Hebrews 13:2

Children, obey your parents. Colossians 3:20

Even a child is known by his doings. Proverbs 20:11

Have peace one with another. Mark 9:50

Hear instruction, and be wise. Proverbs 8:33

Hear, ye children, the instruction of a father. Proverbs 4:1

He that keepeth the law, happy is he. Proverbs 29:18

Honour thy father and thy mother. Exodus 20:12

Keep thy father's commandment, and forsake not the law of thy mother. Proverbs 6:20

Lie not one to another. Colossians 3:9

Love one another. 1 John 4:7

Obey them that have the rule over you. Hebrews 13:17

Use hospitality one to another. 1 Peter 4:9

Wherefore also we make it our aim, whether at home or absent, to be well-pleasing unto him. 2 Corinthians 5:9, ASV

JESUS

And all they that heard it wondered at those things which were told them by the shepherds. Luke 2:18

And he commanded us to preach unto the people, and to testify. Acts 10:42

And they . . . found Mary, and Joseph, and the babe lying in a manger. Luke 2:16

As his custom was, he [Jesus] went into the synagogue on the sabbath day. Luke 4:16

As my Father hath sent me, even so send I you. John 20:21

Fear not: for, behold, I bring you good tidings of great joy. Luke 2:10

For we preach not ourselves, but Christ Jesus the Lord; and ourselves your servants for Jesus' sake. 2 Corinthians 4:5

Glory to God in the highest, and on earth peace, good will toward men. Luke 2:14

God . . . loved us, and sent his Son. 1 John 4:10

God so loved the world, that he gave his only begotten Son, that whosoever believeth in him should not perish, but have everlasting life. John 3:16

Go ye into all the world, and preach the gospel. Mark 16:15

[Jesus said] Go ye therefore, and teach all nations, . . . and, lo, I am with you alway, even unto the end of the world. Matthew 28:19–20

He shall be great, and shall be called the Son of the Highest. Luke 1:32

His name shall be called Wonderful, Counsellor, The mighty God, The everlasting Father, The Prince of Peace. Isaiah 9:6

[Jesus said] Inasmuch as ye have done it unto one of the least of these my brethren, ye have done it unto me. Matthew 25:40

Jesus increased in wisdom and stature, and in favour with God and man. Luke 2:52

Jesus went about all the cities and villages, teaching in their synagogues . . . and healing every sickness and every disease among the people. Matthew 9:35

Jesus . . . went about doing good. Acts 10:38

[Jesus said] Let not your heart be troubled. John 14:1

[Jesus said] Lo, I am with you alway. Matthew 28:20

Lord, teach us to pray. Luke 11:1

The Father sent the Son to be the Saviour of the world. 1 John 4:14

The news about him spread through the whole country of Syria, so that people brought all those who were sick—Jesus healed them all. Matthew 4:24, TEV

These are written, that ye might believe that Jesus is the Christ, the Son of God. John 20:31

This is indeed the Christ, the Saviour of the world. John 4:42

Thou shalt call his name Jesus: for he shall save his people from their sins. Matthew 1:21

Unto you is born this day in the city of David a Saviour, which is Christ the Lord. Luke 2:11

We know that the Son of God is come. 1 John 5:20

When they had opened their treasures, they presented unto him gifts. Matthew 2:11

Ye are my friends, if ye do whatsoever I command you. John 15:14

[Jesus said] Ye shall be witnesses unto me. Acts 1:8

Ye shall find the babe wrapped in swaddling clothes, lying in a manger. Luke 2:12

MISSIONS

And he commanded us to preach unto the people, and to testify. Acts 10:42

And this gospel of the kingdom shall be preached in all the world for a witness unto all nations. Matthew 24:14

As my Father hath sent me, even so send I you. John 20:21

Be ye doers of the word, and not hearers only. James 1:22

Declare his glory among the heathen, his wonders among all people. Psalm 96:3

For we are labourers together with God. 1 Corinthians 3:9

Go ye therefore, and teach all nations, . . . and, lo, I am with you alway, even unto the end of the world. Matthew 28:19–20

How shall they believe in him of whom they have not heard? and how shall they hear without a preacher? and how shall they preach, except they be sent? Romans 10:14–15

[Jesus said] Inasmuch as ye have done it unto one of the least of these my brethren, ye have done it unto me. Matthew 25:40

Let us do good unto all men. Galatians 6:10

Let us not be weary in welldoing. Galatians 6:9

[Love] seeketh not her own. 1 Corinthians 13:5

We . . . are helpers. 2 Corinthians 1:24

We are labourers together with God. 1 Corinthians 3:9

We bring you good tidings. Acts 13:32, ASV

We cannot but speak the things which we have seen and heard. Acts 4:20

[Jesus said] Ye shall be witnesses unto me. Acts 1:8

NATURE

All things were made by him; and without him was not any thing made that was made. John 1:3

And God set them in the firmament of the heaven to give light upon the earth. Genesis 1:17

A river went out . . . to water the garden. Genesis 2:10

For, lo, the winter is past . . . the flowers appear on the earth. Song of Solomon 2:11–12

God created man. Genesis 1:27

God planted a garden. Genesis 2:8

God said, let the earth bring forth the grass, the herb yielding seed, and the fruit tree yielding fruit. Genesis 1:11

[God said] Let there be light. Genesis 1:3

God saw every thing that he had made, and, behold, it was very good. Genesis 1:31

He appointed the moon for seasons. Psalm 104:19

He causeth the grass to grow for the cattle, and herb for the service of man: that he may bring forth food out of the earth. Psalm 104:14

He [God] hath made every thing beautiful. Ecclesiastes 3:11

He [God] maketh the storm a calm, so that the waves thereof are still. Psalm 107:29

He sendeth the springs into the valleys, which run among the hills. Psalms 104:10

In the beginning God created the heaven and the earth. Genesis 1:1

In wisdom hast thou made them all. Psalm 104:24

The hearing ear, and the seeing eye, the Lord hath made even both of them. Proverbs 20:12

The heavens are the work of thy hands. Psalm 102:25

The heavens declare the glory of God; and the firmament shewth his handiwork. Psalm 19:1

The lambs are for thy clothing. Proverbs 27:26

The Lord thinketh upon me. Psalm 40:17

The sea is his, and he made it. Psalm 95:5

The trees of the Lord are full of sap. Psalm 104:16

[God said] The world is mine. Psalm 50:12

They give drink to every beast of the field. Psalm 104:11

Thou hast made summer and winter. Psalm 74:17

While the earth remaineth, seedtime and harvest, and cold and heat, and summer and winter, and day and night shall not cease. Genesis 8:22

OTHERS [GETTING ALONG WITH OTHERS]

A friend loveth at all times. Proverbs 17:17

A man that hath friends must shew himself friendly. Proverbs 18:24

And this is his commandment, That we . . . love one another. 1 John 3:23

A soft answer turneth away wrath. Proverbs 15:1

Be kindly affectioned one to another. Romans 12:10

Be not forgetful to entertain strangers. Hebrews 13:2

Be ye kind one to another, tenderhearted, forgiving one another. Ephesians 4:32

Blessed are the peacemakers: for they shall be called the children of God. Matthew 5:9

By love serve one another. Galatians 5:13

By this shall all men know that ye are my disciples, if ye have love one to another. John 13:35

Do all things without murmurings and disputings. Philippians 2:14

Do for others just what you want them to do for you. Luke 6:31, TEV

Do that which is good, and thou shalt have praise. Romans 13:3

Do that which is honest. 2 Corinthians 13:7

Do those things that are pleasing in his [God's] sight. 1 John 3:22

Forgive, and ye shall be forgiven. Luke 6:37

Freely ye have received, freely give. Matthew 10:8

[God] hath made of one blood all nations of men for to dwell on all the face of the earth. Acts 17:26

God treats all men alike. Acts 10:34, TEV

Have peace one with another. Mark 9:50

Have we not all one father? hath not one God created us? Malachi 2:10

It is more blessed to give than to receive. Acts 20:35

Let us do good unto all men. Galatians 6:10

Let us not love in word, . . . but in deed. 1 John 3:18

Lie not one to another. Colossians 3:9

Live peaceably with all men. Romans 12:18

Love one another. I John 4:7

[Love] seeketh not her own. 1 Corinthians 13:5

Love thy neighbour as thyself. Romans 13:9

Love worketh no ill to his neighbour. Romans 13:10

Love your enemies, bless them that curse you, do good to them that hate you. Matthew 5:44

Love your enemies, bless them that curse you, do good to them that hate you, and pray for them which despitefully use you, and persecute you. Matthew 5:44

Love ye your enemies. Luke 6:35

Love ye therefore the stranger. Deuteronomy 10:19

Obey them that have the rule over you. Hebrews 13:17

Pray one for another. James 5:16

Speak every man truth with his neighbour. Ephesians 4:25

Speak not evil one to another. James 4:11

The disciples decided that each of them would send as much as he could to help their brothers. Acts 11:29, TEV

They helped every one his neighbour. Isaiah 41:6

Thou shalt love the Lord thy God with all thy heart, and with all thy soul, and with all thy mind, and with all thy strength: this is the first commandment. And the second is like, namely this, Thou shalt love thy neighbour as thyself. Mark 12:30–31

Treat men exactly as you would like them to treat you. Luke 6:31, Phillips

Use hospitality one to another. 1 Peter 4:9

PRAISE & WORSHIP

Bring an offering, and come into his courts. Psalm 96:8

Come before his presence with singing. Psalm 100:2

Enter into his gates with thanksgiving, and into his courts with praise. Psalm 100:4

Every man shall give as he is able, according to the blessing of the Lord. Deuteronomy 16:17

Evening, and morning, and at noon, will I pray. Psalm 55:17

For it is written, Thou shalt worship the Lord thy God, and him only shalt thou serve. Matthew 4:10

Freely ye have received, freely give. Matthew 10:8

Give alms of such things as ye have. Luke 11:41

Glorify [praise] God in your body. 1 Corinthians 6:20

Glory to God in the highest, and on earth peace, good will toward men. Luke 2:14

Great is the Lord, and greatly to be praised. Psalm 145:3

God loveth a cheerful giver. 2 Corinthians 9:7

I do always those things that please him. John 8:29

It is a good thing to give thanks unto the Lord, and to sing praises unto thy name, O most High. Psalm 92:1

Lord, teach us to pray. Luke 11:1

Make a joyful noise unto the Lord, all ye lands. Psalm 100:1

Many, O Lord my God, are thy wonderful works which thou hast done. Psalm 40:5

Man ought always to pray. Luke 18:1

My mouth shall speak the praise of the Lord. Psalm 145:21

O come, let us sing unto the Lord. Psalm 95:1

O give thanks unto the Lord; call upon his name: make known his deeds among the people. Psalm 105:1

O give thanks unto the Lord, for he is good. Psalm 107:1

O give thanks unto the Lord; . . . who giveth food to all. Psalm 136:1,25

Oh that men would praise the Lord for his goodness, and for his wonderful works to the children of men! Psalm 107:31

O Lord, how great are thy works! and thy thoughts are very deep. Psalm 92:5

O sing unto the Lord a new song; for he hath done marvellous things. Psalm 98:1

O sing unto the Lord a new song: sing unto the Lord, all the earth. Psalm 96:1

O worship the Lord in the beauty of holiness. Psalm 96:9

Praise ye the Lord. Psalm 149:1

Serve the Lord with gladness: come before his presence with singing. Psalm 100:2

Thanks be unto God for his unspeakable gift. 2 Corinthians 9:15

The heavens declare the glory of God; and the firmament sheweth his handiwork. Psalm 19:1

The Lord hath done great things for us; whereof we are glad. Psalm 126:3

The Lord is good to all: and his tender mercies are over all his works. All thy works shall praise thee, O Lord. Psalm 145:9–10

The Lord is in his holy temple: let all the earth keep silence before him. Habakkuk 2:20

The Lord will hear when I call unto him. Psalm 4:3

This is the day which the Lord hath made; we will rejoice and be glad in it. Psalm 118:24

Thou hast put gladness in my heart. Psalm 4:7

Thou, Lord, art good, and ready to forgive. Psalm 86:5

SELF

All things were made by him; and without him was not any thing made that was made. John 1:3

A merry heart doeth good like a medicine. Proverbs 17:22

And the Lord said unto me, Behold, I have put my words in thy mouth. Jeremiah 1:9

As ye would that men should do to you, do ye also to them. Luke 6:31

A wise son heareth his father's instruction. Proverbs 13:1

Behold, God is mine helper. Psalm 54:4

Be not afraid, . . . for the Lord thy God is with thee. Joshua 1:9

Be strong and of good courage. Deuteronomy 31:6

Be ye doers of the word, and not hearers only. James 1:22

Blessed are the peacemakers: for they shall be called the children of God. Matthew 5:9

Blessed are they that hear the word of God, and keep it. Luke 11:28

But Daniel purposed in his heart that he would not defile himself. Daniel 1:8

By this shall all men know that ye are my disciples, if ye have love one to another. John 13:35

Cease to do evil; learn to do well. Isaiah 1:16–17

Do all things without murmurings and disputings. Philippians 2:14

Do for others just what you want them to do for you. Luke 6:31, TEV

Do good . . . hoping for nothing. Luke 6:35

Do that which is good, and thou shalt have praise. Romans 13:3

Do that which is honest. 2 Corinthians 13:7

Do those things that are pleasing in his [God's] sight. 1 John 3:22

Even a child is known by his doings. Proverbs 20:11

Evening, and morning, and at noon, will I pray. Psalm 55:17

Forgive, and ye shall be forgiven. Luke 6:37

Glorify [praise] God in your body. 1 Corinthians 6:20

God created man. Genesis 1:27

God treats all men alike. Acts 10:34, TEV

Happy is that people, whose God is the Lord. Psalm 144:15

Hear instruction, and be wise. Proverbs 8:33

Hear, ye children, the instruction of a father. Proverbs 4:1

He careth for you. 1 Peter 5:7

He that is faithful in that which is least is faithful also in much. Luke 16:10

He that is slow to anger is better than the mighty. Proverbs 16:32

He that keepth the law, happy is he. Proverbs 29:18

[God says] I am with thee, and will keep thee in all places whither thou goest. Genesis 28:15

I will be glad in the Lord. Psalm 104:34

I will behave myself wisely. Psalm 101:2

I will call upon God; . . . evening, and morning, and at noon, will I pray. Psalm 55:16–17

I will fear no evil: for thou art with me. Psalm 23:4

I will give thanks unto thee, O Lord, . . . I will sing praises unto thy name. 2 Samuel 22:50

I will hear what God the Lord will speak. Psalm 85:8

I will love thee, O Lord. Psalm 18:1

I will not forget thy word. Psalm 119:16

I will praise the name of God with a song. Psalm 69:30

I will sing and give praise. Psalm 108:1

I will sing unto the Lord as long as I live. Psalm 104:33

I will trust, and not be afraid. Isaiah 12:2

Learn to do well. Isaiah 1:17

Let every thing that hath breath praise the Lord. Praise ye the Lord. Psalm 150:6

Lord, be thou my helper. Psalm 30:10

[Love] seeketh not her own. 1 Corinthians 13:5

Love thy neighbour as thyself. Romans 13:9

Love ye your enemies. Luke 6:35

Men ought always to pray. Luke 18:1

My mouth shall speak truth. Proverbs 8:7

My mouth shall speak the praise of the Lord. Psalm 145:21

Pray one for another. James 5:16

Refuse the evil, and choose the good. Isaiah 7:15

Remember all the commandments of the Lord, and do them. Numbers 15:39

Speak every man truth with his neighbour. Ephesians 4:25

Speak not evil one of another. James 4:11

Teach me thy way, O Lord. Psalm 27:11

Teach me to do thy will. Psalm 143:10

The Lord he is God: it is he that hath made us. Psalm 100:3

The Lord is my helper, and I will not fear. Hebrews 13:6

The Lord is the strength of my life; of whom shall I be afraid? Psalm 27:1

The Lord thinketh upon me. Psalm 40:17

The Lord thy God is with thee. Joshua 1:9

The Lord will hear when I call unto him. Psalm 4:3

Then said I, Here am I; send me. Isaiah 6:8

Thou art my help. Psalm 40:17

Thou art near, O Lord; and all thy commandments are true. Psalm 119:151

Thou, Lord, hast made me glad through thy work. Psalm 92:4

Thou, Lord, only makest me dwell in safety. Psalm 4:8

Thou shalt do that which is right. Deuteronomy 12:25

Thou shalt do that which is right and good in the sight of the Lord. Deuteronomy 6:18

Thou shalt love thy neighbour as thyself. Leviticus 19:18

Thou shalt not bear false witness against thy neighbour. Exodus 20:16

Thou shalt not steal. Exodus 20:15

Thou shalt not . . . bear any grudge. Leviticus 19:18

Treat men exactly as you would like them to treat you. Luke 6:31, Phillips

Trust in the Lord, and do good. Psalm 37:3

Use hospitality one to another. 1 Peter 4:9

We . . . are helpers. 2 Corinthians 1:24

We are labourers together with God. 1 Corinthians 3:9

We . . . do those things that are pleasing in his sight. 1 John 3:22

We know that all things work together for good to them that love God. Romans 8:28

We ought to obey God rather than men. Acts 5:29

Whatsoever things were written aforetime were written for our learning. Romans 15:4

Whatsoever thy hand findeth to do, do it with thy might. Ecclesiastes 9:10

Whatsoever ye do in word or deed, do all in the name of the Lord Jesus. Colossians 3:17

Whatsoever ye would that men should do to you, do ye even so to them. Matthew 7:12

Work: for I am with you, saith the Lord. Haggai 2:4

Work with your own hands. 1 Thessalonians 4:11

Ye shall not steal . . . neither lie one to another. Leviticus 4:25